STUDY GUIDE

THE
GLORY
WITHIN

DESTINY IMAGE BOOKS BY COREY RUSSELL

The Glory Within

Ancient Paths

THE GLORY WITHIN

---

*The Interior Life
and the Power of
Speaking in Tongues*

COREY RUSSELL

DESTINY IMAGE® PUBLISHERS, INC.

P.O. Box 310, Shippensburg, PA 17257-0310

"Promoting Inspired Lives."

This book and all other Destiny Image, Revival Press, MercyPlace, Fresh Bread, Destiny Image Fiction, and Treasure House books are available at Christian bookstores and distributors worldwide.

For a U.S. bookstore nearest you, call 1-800-722-6774.

For more information on foreign distributors, call 717-532-3040.

Reach us on the Internet: www.destinyimage.com.

ISBN 13 TP: 978-0-7684-4255-7

For Worldwide Distribution, Printed in the U.S.A.

1 2 3 4 5 6 7 8 / 18 17 16 15 14

CONTENTS

A Note from Corey

To my friends who are getting ready to begin this study—the book *The Glory Within* is very dear to me. This is why it is such an incredible opportunity to share it with you through this eight-week series and help you unlock the power of Holy Spirit on the inside of you.

Just consider this: You have a billion dollars in your spiritual bank account. I'm serious. There is a billion dollars inside of you, just waiting to be withdrawn and released. Why don't we take advantage of this?

A few things immediately come to mind:

- Many of us have forgotten just how glorious our salvation really is;

- The lack of solid, Bible-based teaching on Holy Spirit and His gifts;

- We are unaware of all the amazing benefits of praying in the Holy Spirit.

Seriously, what one item over the last 100-plus years has caused so great a controversy in the church world? Speaking in tongues. Some would say that the controversy is enough reason to avoid the subject completely. I strongly disagree. The greatest controversies surround the greatest truths when it comes to important Kingdom realities. Throughout history, controversy and debate have followed doctrines we uphold as absolutely integral today—the divinity of Christ and the Trinity, to name a few.

I am convinced that the devil stirs up trouble around truth that contains strong potential to dismantle his kingdom. Speaking in tongues and activating the power of Holy Spirit absolutely possesses this power, and in the weeks to come, you will discover why. You will also learn how to access and release this supernatural power in your life!

My goal is that, by the end of our time together, you have a renewed awe of the *glory within*, the Person of the Holy Spirit, and that you are stirred afresh to take your place in a generation that gives itself to activating the glorious gift of praying in tongues.

Corey Russell

Using Your Study Guide

As a participant in the Glory Within curriculum, here is how you will be using this workbook in the weeks ahead:

Video Study Sessions: Whether you are going through these eight lessons in a small group or class or individually, you will be watching the videos and filling in some blanks as you go through the actual sessions (an answer key is located in the back of the workbook). We keep the "fill in the blanks" to a minimum, as we want you to write down the insights that stand out specifically to you and give you the freedom to record what the Holy Spirit shares with you during the sessions.

Daily Reading: There are five daily devotional readings per week. These are designed to reinforce the material you studied and discussed during your actual session. In all, both the readings and answering the discussion questions should not take you more than 15-20 minutes per day.

Glorious Reality: This statement captures the essence of the day's focus.

Daily Discussion Questions: These questions help personalize the material you have been studying, giving you the opportunity to interact with Scripture and the daily reading, along with journaling your own personal reflections.

Prayer: This prayer is totally customizable. In fact, it is designed to be a launching pad for you to enter into your own personal time of conversation with Holy Spirit. More than just studying concepts, principles, and formulas, this curriculum is truly interactive. The goal is not for you to study a bunch of good information; rather, the purpose of it is for you to actually discuss what you are learning with Holy Spirit and ask the

Lord for wisdom, revelation, and direction on how to incorporate these tools into your life.

Week One

UNLOCKING THE GLORY
OF YOUR SALVATION

VIDEO STUDY

1. The greatest miracle is
   your _____.

2. What takes place at your salvation?

   a. You receive God's very _____, infused into your
      spirit.

   b. You experience
      supernatural _____.

   c. You are born of God, and His very _____
      dwells in your spirit.

   d. You become an _____
      sinner.

   e. You receive indestructible, incorruptible life that _____
      the world.

   f. You get positioned to wage successful warfare from this
      position: Christ in _____.

3. We must turn _____ to see the life of
   Christ manifest from without.

THE GREATEST MIRACLE

*"To them God willed to make known what are the riches of the glory of this mystery among the Gentiles: which is Christ in you, the hope of glory." —*Colossians 1:27

JUST LET THAT PHRASE SINK DOWN INTO YOUR HEART RIGHT NOW. "Christ in you." The very Spirit of the Lord Jesus Christ is now living on the inside of you and me, and this Spirit is the hope that we have of the glory to be revealed at His coming. It doesn't get any higher, any deeper, any wider than this revelation crashing into your life. It's this revelation that was hidden for ages and from generations, but has been revealed in these days to you and me. From the very start of this series, we are going to take our time and reflect on this glorious reality that has become ours. I would even invite you to close your eyes and turn within to behold this Man.

This glorious reality is greater than any miracle you will ever experience. Greater than blind eyes popping open, deaf ears popping open, and the dead being raised is the Spirit of this Man, Jesus Christ, coming to live on the inside of you. So many of us who have been believers for a long time have the tendency to bypass the most glorious treasure of all. Our awe and understanding of salvation increases when we slow down and go back to what has been done through Christ's death, resurrection, and ascension. This gift of salvation includes far more than we often consider, such as greater power, intimacy with God, and fruit in our lives.

15

Over the days to come, I am expectant that you are going to come to the realization that the greatest gift you've been looking for is that Person living on the inside of You—waiting to be released through your life. Everything you have desired has already been placed on the inside of you.

GLORIOUS REALITY

The greatest miracle you could ever receive is the supernatural gift of salvation. This inaugurates a brand new reality for you: Christ in you, the hope of glory.

DISCUSSION QUESTIONS

Reflect on your personal salvation experience. What happened? What was it like? How did God introduce Himself to you? (Through this exercise, I want to bring you back to that place where you encountered God for the first time, and help you recapture the glory of your salvation experience.)

_____

_____

_____

_____

_____

PRAYER

Holy Spirit, bring me back to my First Love. Show me the glory of salvation and reignite fresh passion and zeal for what has already been done in my heart.

BEWARE OF OVERFAMILIARITY

"When He had come to His own country, He taught them
in their synagogue, so that they were astonished and said,
'Where did this Man get this wisdom and these mighty works?
Is this not the carpenter's son?'" —Matthew 13:54-55

THIS PORTION OF SCRIPTURE IS A PERFECT EXAMPLE OF HOW MANY OF US consider our salvation—as something familiar. The problem is our familiarity has bred corporate powerlessness. In places where Jesus was simply acknowledged as "the carpenter's son," and treated as a young man who was "familiar" to the community, He was actually restrained from accomplishing powerful miracles. Why? Familiarity has the potential to blind us to the power that is right there before our very eyes.

The same principle is applicable for salvation, and the indwelling Presence of the Holy Spirit within us. Too many of us have become overly familiar with what is nothing less than the most glorious of realities: God breaking down every barrier to ambush humanity with the intention of making our physical bodies the dwelling place of His Holy Spirit. Such truth is nothing short of astonishing. The problem has been a refusal to take a second look at what we would consider to be the "ABCs" of Christianity. And yet, I believe the very key to unlocking the last-days release of glory into the earth has everything to do with believers coming into agreement with what they have already received through conversion.

GLORIOUS REALITY

When we take a second look at realities like being "born again" or "born of God," and then consider their depth and power, salvation becomes a far more glorious gift than we could possibly imagine. The key is breaking down the barrier of familiarity.

DISCUSSION QUESTIONS

Take the next 5-10 minutes and write down what you think of when you read the following terms/phrases:

Born Again

_____

_____

_____

_____

_____

Born of God

_____

_____

_____

_____

_____

New Creation

_____

_____

_____

_____

_____

How does familiarity with the gift of salvation blind us to the power we have received because of our new birth/born again experience?

_____

_____

_____

_____

PRAYER

Holy Spirit, open my eyes to the glory of the gift of salvation I have received in Christ. Help me to identify and confront any familiarity that has crept in and diluted my awe of this wondrous reality.

I'M A NEW CREATION

*"Therefore if any person is [ingrafted] in Christ (the Messiah)
he is a new creation (a new creature altogether); the old [previ-
ous moral and spiritual condition] has passed away. Behold,
the fresh and new has come!"* —2 Corinthians 5:17 AMP

A NEW CREATION WITH A NEW NATURE, A NEW INTIMACY WITH GOD, A
new power over sin, and a new destiny is what happened the moment you
and I received Jesus into our life as our Lord and savior. What happened
in Genesis 1, as great and magnificent as it is, is not as great as what
God did when He came to live inside you and me. I love the word *new*,
because Paul is letting us know that you and I, "in Christ," are something
the world has never seen before—new creations.

The moment that Adam sinned he died a spiritual death. The life
of God within him left, and slowly his body followed. Through Christ's
death and resurrection and outpouring of the Spirit, that life has now
returned and you and I will never die. Death's sting has been destroyed
and the curse of sin has been broken over us who are "in Him." Though
we may die physically, we will be raised again, putting on immortal life,
and will live and reign forever with Him.

You are a new creation being prepared for a new heaven and a new
earth. What's on inside of you right now is reserved for the ages to come.
In Revelation 21, God Himself said, "Behold, I make all things new."
This is God's heart and God's purpose, and everything He is doing is

about making everything new, and He began with us and our relationship with Him. Today, I want you to lean back, take a deep breath, and begin to repeat the phrase, "I'm a new creation in Christ. The old is gone and the new has come."

GLORIOUS REALITY

In Christ, you and I are a "new creation" with a new nature, new desires, new intimacy, and new power over the devil and sin.

DISCUSSION QUESTIONS

What are some of the phrases and thoughts that come to your mind as you consider that you are new creation?

_____

_____

_____

_____

_____

What do you think life will look like when we are dwelling on the new earth with a new heaven?

_____

_____

_____

_____

_____

Does this change the way you view your salvation? Explain.

_____

_____

_____

_____

_____

_____

_____

PRAYER

Holy Spirit, help me to understand what it looks like to think and live as an entirely new creation!

THE SEED OF GOD LIVES INSIDE OF YOU

"Whoever has been born of God does not sin, for His seed remains in him; and he cannot sin, because he has been born of God." —1 John 3:9

THIS IS ONE OF THOSE INTENSE PASSAGES THAT SCARE A LOT OF US, BUT in my opinion it is what one of the clearest "litmus test" verses over whether or not someone is saved. John is making it clear that whoever has been born of God will never be a successful sinner. I don't know about you, but after I was born again, I tried to do some things that previously, I did with no regret at all, but after I was born again, I thought I was falling into hell. The very feelings of regret, conviction, and fear were actually signs that I was born of God and that I was a son of God. If you are struggling with areas of sin and are pained over it to the point of being willing to do something about it, know that you are experiencing the life of God in you. I would tell people to fear when they go months and years without any sense of remorse over their current state in God. Again, when we come into Christ, we are a new creation with a new nature and new desires. The man who has been born of God has a harder time being a successful sinner than a cat does barking. The two realities don't go together. Know this—that if you are warring against areas of sin in your life, you are loved by God. You are a lover of God who is struggling with sin, not a sinner who is struggling to love God. The difference between those two is huge.

The next phrase of this verse is absolutely astounding. God's seed *remains in him.* The very DNA seed of the eternal God is living in you right now. What this simply means is that in the same way your parents' DNA resides within you and you carry and exemplify similar traits, characteristics, body types, hair color, nose, ears, etc., so it is with God. His DNA lives in you and as you grow in Him, His life and His character will be formed in and through you and you will begin to look like His Son.

GLORIOUS REALITY

When you got born again, the very seed of God took up residence inside of your spirit. This seed is the Holy Spirit, and His mission is to produce the character traits and attributes of God in your life.

DISCUSSION QUESTIONS

In what ways do you see a comparison between us being *born of God*, and the character traits and attributes a child inherits from his/her natural parents?

_____

_____

_____

_____

_____

How does the indwelling Presence of Holy Spirit make living in perpetual sin difficult for a believer? How have you experienced this in your personal walk with the Lord?

_____

_____

_____

_____

_____

Prayer

Thank You, Holy Spirit, that You are producing the characteristics and attributes of the Living God in and through me.

BORN AGAIN TO SEE
THE KINGDOM

"Jesus answered and said to him, 'Most assur-
edly, I say to you, unless one is born again, he can-
not see the kingdom of God.'" —John 3:3

DON'T YOU LOVE JESUS? NICODEMUS CAME TO HIM AT NIGHT AND through flattery was trying to win Jesus over. Jesus cut through all the politics and flattery, and in essence said, "You don't have a clue who I am and how to enter My Kingdom unless you are born again." What was it like for this educated ruler of the Pharisees to hear that unless he was born again, he couldn't see or enter the Kingdom of God? Jesus brought this brilliant theologian who prided himself in spiritual matters to a bumbling fool asking questions about having to enter back into his mother's stomach to be born again.

There is a natural birth and then there is a spiritual birth that opens us up to a whole new world, a whole new Kingdom. When we are born again, that which we were blind to before we are now able to perceive and understand, because we are new people. That conversion process requires great humility and awareness that I'm in need of something and Someone outside of myself.

We see everything differently. We see ourselves differently. We see our value, our worth, and our destiny differently. Eternity becomes the most real thing in the world. We see God differently. He goes from a faraway person to a relational, very present Person whom we can turn to at any time with any problem. We see other people differently. We love those we could not stand before. We see God's creation differently. I remember sitting on my swing on my front porch just hours after I experienced salvation. I remember looking at the sky and being undone by how blue the sky was, how green the grass was, and how loud the birds were chirping. It was like I had been dead for 20 years and was suddenly alive. And at that moment it hit me—I'm alive!

GLORIOUS REALITY

When we are born again, we see the Kingdom of God.

DISCUSSION QUESTIONS

Read John 3:1-21. How was Nicodemus trying to understand the "born again" experience that Jesus was describing?

_____

_____

_____

_____

What role does the Holy Spirit play in the "born again" experience? (verses 5-8)

_____

_____

_____

_____

How has this week increased your gratitude and awe for your salvation?

_____

_____

_____

_____

_____

PRAYER

Holy Spirit, thank You for overcoming every barrier and obstacle to bring me into the Kingdom. Continue to open my eyes—and at the same time, awe my heart—to the wondrous realities that are available to me to experience and release to the world, living in this Kingdom, and having You within me.

Week Two

Rediscovering Holy Spirit: God on the Inside of You

Video Study

Who Is Holy Spirit?

1. Holy Spirit is a _____.

2. Holy Spirit is _____.

3. Holy Spirit _____ our relationship with God.

4. Holy Spirit is
    our _____.

5. Holy Spirit is the Spirit
    of _____.

6. Holy Spirit lives with
    us _____.

7. Holy Spirit is
    our _____.

What Will Holy Spirit Do?

1. He will _____ you into all truth.

2. He will not speak on His
    own _____.

3. He will tell you things to _____.

4. He will glorify_____.

5. He will take the things that belong to Jesus and _____
    them to you.

Who Is Holy Spirit?

1. Holy Spirit knows and reveals the _____ things
    of God.

2. Holy Spirit is the down payment and guarantee of
    the _____.

YOUR UPGRADE

*"Nevertheless I tell you the truth. It is to your advantage that
I go away; for if I do not go away, the Helper will not come to
you; but if I depart, I will send Him to you."* —John 16:7

THIS WEEK, I WANT US TO START LOOKING AT THE REALITY OF HOW THIS
hope in glory is experienced. It's obvious that Jesus the Man does not live
inside of us, so we have to ask ourselves: *What does Christ in me look like?*
John 13–17 powerfully help us answer this question, as they are absolutely revolutionary chapters of Scripture when it comes to introducing
the Person and purpose of Holy Spirit. In fact, I am going to include
some daily Scripture readings this week in the discussion questions, with
excerpts from these chapters, as well as 1 Corinthians 2.

First, I want you to recognize the *upgrade* of Holy Spirit. Did you
know that what you possess inside of you is actually an advantage beyond
what the disciples experienced, even in proximity to the Person of Jesus
Christ? I have to believe that what Jesus said in John 16:7 was absolutely
mind blowing to them. "How could there be an *advantage* beyond having
You here?" Surely thoughts like this raced through their minds. The
reality is, Holy Spirit was contained in the body of one Man while Jesus
was on the earth. Because of the Cross, and ultimately, Pentecost, this
same Spirit would be released to *all* who would call upon the Name of the
Lord, generation after generation, spanning the globe. Are you beginning
to see the *upgrade* you've received in Holy Spirit?

GLORIOUS REALITY

You have access to a relationship with God that even the disciples didn't experience, for now God lives inside of you in the Person of Holy Spirit and He is not limited to just one person.

DISCUSSION QUESTIONS

Read John 16:5-15. How would the Holy Spirit be an *advantage* and *upgrade* to the disciples?

_____

_____

_____

_____

_____

Why was it necessary for Jesus to leave?

_____

_____

_____

_____

_____

In what ways can you enjoy a relationship with God *greater* than even those who lived at the time of Jesus?

_____

_____

_____

_____

_____

PRAYER

Holy Spirit, thank You for upgrading my relationship with the Father and for depositing Your very Presence into my spirit. Help me understand and access every advantage of this new level of intimacy.

PERSON, FORCE, OR THING?

"...But if I depart, I will send Him to you." —John 16:7

FROM HERE ON OUT, I WANT TO CONSISTENTLY IDENTIFY HOLY SPIRIT *without* a "the" introducing Him. Just as my name is Corey Russell, His Name is Holy Spirit. He is not a force field, a fuzzy, or a feeling, He is a Person. In the same way we don't talk about Jesus as *the Jesus*, we should likewise consider Holy Spirit, as He is equally a person. This is one of the reasons I am convinced more people do not actually enjoy the advantage of relationship with Holy Spirit. It is easy to have relationship with a Person; it is another thing to try and have relationship with a force or even a power source. We will respond to Holy Spirit based on how we see Him—correctly or incorrectly. If we see Holy Spirit as some type of force or divine energy, then we will resist engaging Him in relationship as we would the Father or Jesus.

Again, it is easy to have relationship with One identified as the Father or Son, but the *Spirit*? I want to encourage you to shift the way you view Holy Spirit, for He is just as much God, and just as much a Person as the Father and Son. Before your relationship goes to a new level, and you begin to interact with Him differently, it is absolutely key that first and foremost you see and treat Him like a Person. I guarantee you, once that perspective shift takes place, your relationship with Him will go to a whole other level.

GLORIOUS REALITY

Holy Spirit is not an impersonal force or energy source—He is just as much a Person as both the Father and Jesus, and you can enjoy relationship with Him in the same way.

DISCUSSION QUESTIONS

How does our perspective on Holy Spirit determine how we relate with Him?

_____

_____

_____

_____

_____

Why is it so important that we view Holy Spirit as a Person?

_____

_____

_____

_____

_____

How have you interacted with Holy Spirit in the past? How does this truth of Him being a Person impact your relationship with Him today?

_____

_____

_____

_____

_____

PRAYER

Holy Spirit, help me to correct any incorrect views I have about You. You are a Glorious Person whom I have the joy of knowing, fellowshipping with, talking with, and listening to. Thank You for taking our relationship to new levels in the days ahead!

WHAT WILL HE DO?

"When He, the Spirit of truth, has come, He will guide you into all truth; for He will not speak on His own authority, but whatever He hears He will speak; and He will tell you things to come. He will glorify Me, for He will take of what is Mine and declare it to you." —John 16:13-14

JESUS TELLS US THAT WHEN HOLY SPIRIT COMES, HE WILL DO SEVERAL things. He will guide you into all truth. He will not speak on His own authority, and He will speak whatever He hears. He will tell you things to come. He will glorify Jesus. He will take the things that belong to Jesus and declare them to you. What a job description! The clearer we get on who He is, where He lives, and what He does, the clearer our relationship will become.

Holy Spirit's job description is to guide us. He does this by the still small voice within. He does this by highlighting the word of God. He does this through dreams and visions. He does this through other people. His desire is to bring you into all truth, and truth is a Person. His name is Jesus. Holy Spirit is submitted to the Father and the Son and will speak (to those who have ears to hear) whatever He is hearing. I love to ask Holy Spirit, "What are You hearing, Holy Spirit?" Holy Spirit will tell you what's coming. He will do this for you individually. He will tell you what's coming with friends, family, churches, cities, nations, globally. He is a prophet and He will tell you what's coming. His whole aim is glorifying Jesus. To those who care to take the time, He will take the things that belong to Jesus and make them known to you. I would encourage you to turn within, focus on the indwelling Holy Spirit, and begin to ask Him to guide you, to speak to you, to open up your understanding. I promise that He will answer you!

GLORIOUS REALITY

When Holy Spirit comes, He does not bring disorder and chaos. He teaches, communicates, declares, and glorifies Jesus.

DISCUSSION QUESTIONS

Reread John 16:12-15. Which of these six descriptions of Holy Spirit is your favorite? Why? How has this been played out in your life?

_____

_____

_____

_____

_____

How have you personally experienced the ways of the Holy Spirit described in John 16:12-15?

_____

_____

_____

_____

PRAYER

Holy Spirit, I ask You to be my Teacher. I invite You to let me in on what the Father is saying. You are welcome to show me things to come and reveal to me what Jesus has been speaking since the beginning. In all things, glorify Jesus in my life as I continue to know and encounter You in deeper ways.

THE PERSON WHO KNOWS GOD BEST

"For the Spirit searches all things, yes, the deep things of God. For what man knows the things of a man except the spirit of the man which is in him? Even so no one knows the things of God except the Spirit of God. Now we have received, not the spirit of the world, but the Spirit who is from God, that we might know the things that have been freely given to us by God." —1 Corinthians 2:10-12

IN MY OPINION, THIS IS SOME OF THE CLEAREST DEFINITION TO THE JOB description of Holy Spirit. Paul makes several amazing statements, beginning with the first one. "The Spirit searches all things." I love the word *search*. I don't know about you, but I absolutely love Google. I love being able to type in a name or a phrase and getting access to hundreds, sometimes thousands of websites that either contain that information or are connected to that name. And the thing that blows me away is that it's a human-made search engine! What does the search engine of heaven know of the things of God? What does Holy Spirit know about Jesus our Bridegroom, God our Father, our King, our Creator? How many verses and thoughts and phrases does Holy Spirit have concerning God Himself? It's my lifelong pursuit to find out what Holy Spirit knows about God.

He searches the deep things of God. What are the "deep things of God"? I've got to know and I won't stop until I find out.

My favorite part of this verse is that these "deep things" that the Holy Spirit searches out concerning God are not for some elite group off in the desert, but are for simple everyday people like you and me with no special abilities, giftings, or influence. Our inheritance is to know the deep things of God. Jesus said in Matthew 13 that it's been given to us to know the mysteries of the Kingdom. Our inheritance is for Holy Spirit to take the things that belong to God and make them known to you and me. When the Spirit of revelation touches our hearts, nothing can stop us. We love more, give more, believe more, and sacrifice more when those deep things are made known to us. Let's ask Him today for them!

GLORIOUS REALITY

Holy Spirit is the search engine of heaven.

DISCUSSION QUESTIONS

Read 1 Corinthians 2:6-16. What do you think it means for Holy Spirit to search out the deep things of God?

_____

_____

_____

_____

How much do you *ask* Holy Spirit certain truths about God and His Word? Are there any concepts, truths, or accounts in Scripture that you currently need clarity on? If so, dialogue with Holy Spirit about these things and write down what He reveals.

_____

_____

_____

_____

_____

_____

_____

PRAYER

Holy Spirit, You are glorious. You are the only One who knows God in a greater, deeper way than any other. You are a faithful, accurate Witness of who God is, what He's like, and what He's doing.

WHO IS HE SHARING WITH?

"But as it is written: 'Eye has not seen, nor ear heard, nor have entered into the heart of man the things which God has prepared for those who love Him.' But God has revealed them to us through His Spirit." —1 Corinthians 2:9-10

I LOVE THIS VERSE. I LOVE THAT THERE ARE THINGS THAT NO EYE HAS ever seen, or no ear has ever heard, or the fact that there are things that have never entered the heart of man. That by itself is amazing, but Paul continues and adds a little something to Isaiah's prophecy by saying that none of those things have dawned on the eyes, ears, and hearts of the ones who love God. Do you love God? Well, if you do, then this verse gives you a sneak peak of what eternity will look like. God has eternity to set up billions of years of surprises for you and me. He will be freshly blowing our minds with discoveries of who He is, who we are, what He has done, and what He will do. This is absolutely amazing!

Ephesians 2:7 tells us, *"that in the ages to come He might show the exceeding riches of His grace in His kindness toward us in Christ Jesus."* For the next billion years, God will be showing you and me off as the trophies of His grace and kindness in raising us up and seating us with His Son. We will never "get over" the fact that God has sent His Son to the earth to become a Man, live the life we could never live, die our death, and then raise us up with Himself from the dead and seat us together with Himself.

Paul then goes on to say that God has revealed these realities of eternity to us now by the Spirit who lives within us. Beloved, you have the powers of the age to come living on the inside of you right now. Drink today of eternity and be filled!

GLORIOUS REALITY

It has not even dawned on your eyes, ears, and heart what God has prepared for you who love Him.

DISCUSSION QUESTIONS

What do you think eternity will be like and how will God surprise you?

_____

_____

_____

_____

_____

What does it mean that now the Spirit lives in you, carrying the glories of the age to come?

_____

_____

_____

_____

_____

PRAYER

Holy Spirit, thank You for opening up the realm of mystery and sharing the deep things of God with me. I understand that now I still see and hear in part. At the same time, I also thank You that You do speak, You do share, You do reveal, and You do let us in on who the Father is, what He is saying, and what He is doing.

Week Three

KEYS TO ENJOYING DEEPER COMMUNION WITH HOLY SPIRIT

VIDEO STUDY

God's Divine Design for Communion:

1. God designed you for _____ with Himself.

2. God designed the Old Testament _____ to experience intimacy with His people.

3. God made a way for _____ to become His temple and dwelling place.

4. God designed you to be like His _____.

Three Keys to Understanding God's Design for Communion. You Have:

1. An _____ _____: The natural, visible realm.

2. An inner court: Your _____, consisting of mind, will, and emotions.

3. The Holy of Holies: In the deep of your _____.

How You Can Experience Communion with Holy Spirit

1. God wanted to build a _____ that could handle His Presence.

2. Through Jesus' blood, you have become God's _____ dwelling place.

3. You hear God's voice to the degree that you _____ with Holy Spirit.

4. We must stop living _____ the inheritance we have received in Holy Spirit.

Tools to Experience Holy Spirit in Your Life:

1. _____ on the Word of God. _____ are the doorway into revelation.

2. _____ with Holy Spirit.

TRUST

- T_____ Holy Spirit.

- R_____ in me, Holy Spirit.

- U_____ me, Holy Spirit.

- S_____ me, Holy Spirit.

- T_____ me, Holy Spirit.

Day One

You Were Created for Divine Fellowship

"Then God said, 'Let Us make man in Our image, according to Our likeness…'" —Genesis 1:26

GOD MADE YOU IN HIS IMAGE AND LIKENESS. HE CREATED YOU FOR Himself, for deep intimacy and communion. Nothing else in creation was fashioned in such a way. From the animals to the plant life, all other forms of the living created order were *not* made to where they could actually be compatible with God. This was His intent from the very beginning for man. He created us with internal capacities to relate with God spirit to Spirit and with the capacity and ability to represent Him to the rest of the created order. The very first thing God did after creating Adam was plant a garden. He then put Adam in the garden and gave him the command to tend and cultivate this garden, because this would be the place God would come meet with him and fill him with the knowledge of His will.

God's desire through the Old Testament is that He would dwell among us and us with Him. This is what He wants. David caught this vision and gave his life to the fulfillment of it when he cried out, *"I will not give sleep to my eyes or slumber to my eyelids, until I find a place for the Lord, a dwelling place for the Mighty One of Jacob"* (Ps. 132:4-5).

When approaching the subject of Holy Spirit, you must settle it: God wants to be as close to you as possible. It's His desire. It's His longing.

Jesus prayed in John 17:24, *"Father I desire that they also whom You gave Me may be with Me where I am."* That's what He wants. That's why He created us. That's why He died, and that's why He's coming again.

GLORIOUS REALITY

God created you for deep intimacy, communion, and partnership with His plans and purposes.

DISCUSSION QUESTIONS

Read Genesis 1:26. What does it mean that you were made in *God's image* and *likeness?* Why do you think it was important?

_____

_____

_____

_____

How does it make you feel to be so pursued by the God of heaven?

_____

_____

_____

_____

PRAYER

Holy Spirit, You have made it possible for me to fellowship with God and enjoy intimate communion with Him. Thank You for bringing me into this rich place of fellowship, and thank You for living inside of me.

Day Two

AN OLD TESTAMENT
SHADOW OF COMMUNION

*"Do you not know that you are the temple of God and that
the Spirit of God dwells in you?"* —1 Corinthians 3:16

GOD'S DILEMMA HAS ALWAYS BEEN FILLING A STRUCTURE THAT HE DOESN'T destroy when He manifests Himself. Every time God shows up, buildings start shaking, mountains start quaking, heavens start moving because the eternal, infinite God steps down into our little world and it can barely handle His glory. When Isaiah saw the Lord in the temple, the posts of the door were shaken. When God showed up on Sinai, no one could even touch the mountain or they would die. When God designed the human body, He answered this dilemma by creating a structure that could contain His glory and not be destroyed by it. You need to thank God that there isn't smoke coming out of your ears right now or that you actually didn't blow up in your sleep last night! Paul affirms this reality when he told the Corinthians, "You are the temple of God." Through the shed blood of Jesus Christ, you have been cleansed and made a suitable dwelling place for His Spirit.

In the Old Testament, we see God relating to man in different ways. We see Him coming to man and being with man, but in the New Testament, we see God in man. This is absolutely astounding as we consider that the God of Sinai, the God of the Red Sea, the God of Genesis 1 has made you and me His home through the death, resurrection, and ascension of Jesus Christ. Today, I encourage you to consider the fact that the veil of separation has been removed and through Holy Spirit, God lives in you right now.

GLORIOUS REALITY

The same Spirit of God that dwelt in the tabernacle of Moses and temple of Solomon lives on the inside of you.

DISCUSSION QUESTIONS

Why do you think it is important to return to the Old Testament in order to understand what we have received, in full, because of Christ's work?

_____

_____

_____

_____

_____

When you think about *who* lives on the inside of you (in light of the *temple of God* description in 1 Corinthians 3:16), what does this do to your relationship with Holy Spirit?

_____

_____

_____

_____

_____

PRAYER

Holy Spirit, you dwelt in the tabernacle of Moses and in the temple of Solomon. You are the Shekinah Glory and the very Presence of God, and You dwell inside of me. Thank You for taking up residence in my spirit and for making my body Your temple.

Day Three

YOU ARE HOLY SPIRIT'S DWELLING PLACE

"For you are the temple of the living God. As God has said: 'I will dwell in them and walk among them. I will be their God, and they shall be My people.'" —2 Corinthians 6:16

IN YESTERDAY'S STUDY AND TODAY'S, WE SEE THE TWO DIFFERENT TIMES that Paul calls us the temple of the living God. In each of these verses, the larger context is Paul calling the Corinthians out of sin. I think it's amazing how the apostle Paul reminds these believers that they are the temple of the living God as the motivator to not allow any sin to dwell in them. One of the greatest motivations in my life to live holy is knowing that God has given me His very depth, His very life. When I consider this investment in me, it causes such gratitude and care to protect this at all costs. Have you ever walked around with a lot of cash in your pockets? How do you walk? I've had lots of cash in my pockets before and when it's there, I put it all in the front pockets and usually have my hands either on or in my pockets. Why do I do this? Because of the value of money that is on me! What if we cared for the life of God within us by what we look at, listen to, talk about, engage with?

Holy Spirit's first name is Holy, and the more and more that we grow in understanding of who He is and how utterly amazing it is that this Person has made you His home, the greater our desire to guard this relationship at all costs will be. We know from Ephesians 5 that Holy Spirit

65

can be grieved by the way we talk. I've experienced firsthand Holy Spirit being grieved from what I've looked at or what I've listened to, and when this has touched me I've set my heart to never purposely do anything to harm our relationship. Today, I want you to turn within and behold that living flame dwelling deep within you and ask Him to reveal any areas that have or could potentially affect your relationship. I've settled it that intimacy and communion with Holy Spirit is the greatest way to live.

GLORIOUS REALITY

Holy Spirit lives within us, thereby empowering us to say no to all forms of sin.

DISCUSSION QUESTION

Are there any areas in your life that you believe are hindering your relationship with Holy Spirit? Please list and discuss.

_____

_____

_____

_____

_____

Take some time today to meditate on the glory of God residing within you.

_____

_____

_____

_____

_____

Prayer

Holy Spirit, increase my awareness of the glorious gift I have received in You. I say no to all forms of sin. I will guard Your investment in me with all my heart, soul, mind, and strength.

Day Four

WORD AND SPIRIT: YOU CAN'T HAVE ONE WITHOUT THE OTHER

"The words that I speak to you are spirit, and they are life" —John 6:63

OVER THE NEXT TWO DAYS, I WANT US TO FOCUS ON ONE OF THE KEY ways that we fellowship with Holy Spirit—*meditation on the Word of God.* As I have said before, we cannot divorce the Spirit and the Word. The two are one and the same Person, and you cannot have one without the other. As we seek to grow in deeper intimacy with Holy Spirit, know right now that Holy Spirit's favorite chariot to ride in is the Word of God. There is no greater place of Holy Spirit encounter than in long and loving meditation in the Word of God, and there is no greater place of encountering truth than when talking to Holy Spirit. He is called the Spirit of Truth. Learning how to receive the "spirit" of Jesus' words is the journey we are on. In John 6, Jesus pulled out the "eat My flesh and drink My blood" teaching. This was a very hard teaching and caused many people to turn away and stop following because they didn't understand His language. Jesus is making it clear that He is not advocating cannibalism, but is calling them to feed on His words as their life.

Next week, we are going to begin to shift this series into the glory and power of speaking in tongues. I've found that the greatest way to enhance my times of praying in tongues is meditating in the Word of

God. I've seen many people get weird when they speak in tongues all the time, but have no life or depth in the Word of God. I've also seen people who know a lot of Bible verses, but are dry as bones because they are not intimate with the Spirit of the Word. As you read the word, slow down and quietly repeat phrases back to God that are sticking out to you. Lightly intermingle praying in the spirit as you read. As phrases increase, write them down and just keep reading. Your life will never be the same!

GLORIOUS REALITY

As we come before the Word of God, set your heart to receive and encounter the Spirit of God being breathed through the Word of God.

DISCUSSION QUESTIONS

What are some practical ways you have found to slow down and encounter Holy Spirit through reading the Word of God?

_____

_____

_____

_____

_____

Have you been guilty of choosing one—the Word or the Spirit—over the other? If so, describe *why* you went with one over the other.

_____

_____

_____

_____

_____

PRAYER

Holy Spirit, You are my guide and Teacher. I don't want to just read words on a page so I can have more information. I thank You, Holy Spirit, that You take Scripture and bring it to life so that I can experience the supernatural transformation that I read about.

THE GREATEST BIBLE TEACHER ON THE PLANET

*"But the anointing which you have received from
Him abides in you, and you do not need that anyone teach you...."* —1 John 2:27

DID YOU KNOW THAT THERE IS AN ANOINTING THAT LIVES INSIDE OF you? You have received the anointing that teaches you, guides you, and reveals the Word of God to you. No matter how small or ungifted you feel, there is an anointing on the inside of you.

I believe it is important to build on the truth we focused on yester-day, as this is a much-needed area of breakthrough in all of our personal walks with Holy Spirit. We *must* start accessing what we have received in the Person of Holy Spirit. *He is* that wonderful anointing on the inside of us, awaiting communion. In the verse above, the apostle John takes our concept of Bible study to a whole new level when he tells us that the anointing we have received in the Person of Holy Spirit makes it possible to be taught, led, directed, guided, and empowered by the Spirit.

Jesus Himself said that *"the Helper, the Holy Spirit, whom the Father will send in My name...will teach you all things"* (John 14:26). I am blown away by the phrase "all things." Are you struggling in your Bible study time? Is it boring, stale, and dry? Do you feel like you are just reading words on a page and doing your best to get through to the next chapter? I encourage you, invite Holy Spirit into the process. The anointing He gives shines a supernatural light on Scripture, opening your eyes to new understanding as you actually study the Bible *with* Holy Spirit.

I've written a book entitled *Ancient Paths: Rediscovering Delight in the Word of God.* In this book, I talk about ways to move out of boredom into a place of delight in the Word of God. As you read, slow down, and as verses touch you, turn them into prayers back to God. Lightly intermingle praying in the spirit and short prayers. He will help you and teach you as you go. The Word of God is starting a conversation. It's more than a duty or discipline. It's a conversation with a Person.

GLORIOUS REALITY

Since Holy Spirit wrote the Word, He is the greatest Teacher when it comes to Scripture. We don't need to completely depend on someone else to receive our revelation about God; Holy Spirit is our great escort in Bible study, showing us Who God is, answering the questions we have, and helping us understand things we are struggling with.

REFLECTION

I encourage you to pray the TRUST acronym right now, inviting Holy Spirit into your experience and understanding of God's Word.

> **T**alk with me, Holy Spirit.
> **R**eign in me, Holy Spirit.
> **U**se me, Holy Spirit.
> **S**trengthen me, Holy Spirit.
> **T**each me, Holy Spirit.

I want to encourage you to start making your Bible study/devotional time interactive with Holy Spirit. He wants to answer questions, break familiarity, reveal fresh truth about Jesus, and bring the Word of God to life for you.

Prayer

Holy Spirit, I invite You to take my Bible study to the next level. Reading words on a page is not enough. Depending on and feeding off of other people's revelation about God is not enough. I appreciate it and learn from it, but I want my own dynamic, intimate relationship with You. Thank You for revealing mysteries, for answering questions, and for unveiling Jesus in greater ways than I could experience in my own strength and intellect.

Week Four

The Importance of Speaking in Tongues

VIDEO STUDY

Truths About Speaking in Tongues:

1. The devil doesn't spend time on things that don't _____ his kingdom.

2. Tongues are a key _____ into the prophetic spirit.

3. Praying in tongues opens up your _____ gift.

4. Praying in tongues opens up _____ in a new way.

5. Praying in tongues was a major part of Paul's _____ life.

6. Praying in tongues reveals a supernatural _____ of God.

7. Speaking in tongues birthed the _____.

Three Expressions of Tongues in the New Testament:

1. Speaking in actual _____ that are unknown to the speaker.

2. A corporate _____ of tongues that brings edification and strength to the church.

3. A personal, private _____ language available to all believers.

It's Legal to Desire Spiritual Gifts

*"Earnestly desire and cultivate the spiritual endow-
ments (gifts)...."* —1 Corinthians 14:1 AMP

THE FIRST THREE WEEKS WERE DEDICATED TO ESTABLISHING A FOUNDA-
tion to build on. We've looked at the glorious reality of our salvation,
the identity of the One who lives inside of us, and some of the ways
to fellowship with Holy Spirit. Now, I want to focus on the key cata-
lyst for communion that we will be discussing throughout the rest of
this series—tongues. The first thing I want to do is completely clear the
air, and invite you into a wholehearted pursuit of the fullness of God
being experienced and released in your life. As we will learn, the apostle
Paul knew something about spiritual gifts, and particularly speaking in
tongues. He was not ashamed of it, but on the contrary, invited all believers to *earnestly desire and cultivate* these realities in our lives

I'm coming to realize that the very thing that the Charismatic church
is known for—speaking in tongues—is the very practice it engages the
least. Many have received a touch from Holy Spirit, been baptized in the
Spirit, spoke in tongues, and then memorialized the experience. We treat
it like our spiritual badge. "I got that," or "I had that happen to me," or
"I spoke in tongues." Whether we spoke in tongues has little meaning
when it comes to *today*. I want to stir you to not only return to the place

of praying in tongues, but I want to give you a vision for extended times of praying in tongues. Many of us have reduced this experience to falling down at the altar with these languages coming out of us, but I want to give you a vision for praying in tongues when you wake up, when you are driving to school or work, when you are doing the dishes, when you are at the grocery store, and in many other ways and places. In this way, you as the temple of God are living a life of unceasing prayer. This should not be considered taboo, back room stuff. Paul spent a great deal of time focusing on this practice of believers praying in a personal prayer language. Why? Little keys open up big doors. I believe praying in tongues is a gateway to the other gifts of the Spirit, the fruit of the Spirit, and power of the Spirit.

GLORIOUS REALITY

Praying in tongues will usher you into a whole new life of intimacy and power with God.

DISCUSSION QUESTIONS

Why do you think the subject of tongues has been such a difficult topic for so many in the Body of Christ?

_____

_____

_____

_____

_____

_____

_____

_____

Before we move forward, pause and consider "where you stand" on tongues. Honestly write down your thoughts in the space below. (Examples: spoke in tongues once and don't anymore; never received it; do it once and a while, etc.)

_____

_____

_____

_____

_____

_____

_____

_____

_____

There might be an element of conviction that arises for not engaging this wonderful gift. God is not mad about it, nor is this a matter of feeling condemned. It's simply time to reopen this amazing gift and start stewarding it.

PRAYER

Holy Spirit, I want everything You have for me. I pursue Your gifts with passion, desiring to experience their activation in my life. They are not badges of honor. They are not designed to make me appear more spiritual. They are for my edification and for the strengthening of Your body!

A GLIMPSE INTO APOSTLE PAUL'S DEVOTIONAL LIFE

"I thank God that I speak in tongues more than any of you." —1 Corinthians 14:18 NLT

WHEN IT COMES TO FORERUNNERS IN THE FAITH WHO HAVE BLAZED trails and accomplished mighty exploits for the Kingdom, the apostle Paul stands out above the rest. The very man who wrote the majority of the New Testament and helped spread the Gospel across the known world says that he spoke in tongues more than the rest of the Corinthian church. This is amazing! I've asked myself the question many times: How could the busiest, most effective, most powerful apostle make such a bold statement to the Corinthian church? How could the man who exemplified the character of Christ, the love of Christ, and the power of Christ say such a bold statement? Here is, in my opinion, the clearest window into his personal devotional life. This was a man who was undeniably sold out to the Holy Spirit and grateful for His gifts and I believe his example invites us to make a decision. Paul's example refuses to let us remain "on the fence" about praying in tongues.

The Message version phrases 1 Corinthians 14:18 this way, *"I'm grateful to God for the gift of praying in tongues that he gives us for praising him, which leads to wonderful intimacies we enjoy with him."* I enter into this as much or more than any of you. I pray these words are even now awakening you to know and experience God in the way that Paul did. Could it be that the "secret" to intimacy and power that you've been looking for is found in that gift you received years ago, but have not really engaged with?

I'm convinced that as we begin to give ourselves to extended times of praying in tongues, we will see the destinies and breakthroughs that we've been looking for start to come forth. His experience was not isolated and restricted only to him—a "super apostle." He modeled something accessible and available to each one of us today; otherwise, he would not have shared such detailed instruction on it. If Paul was grateful for the gift of praying in tongues, I propose that it is something we need to pursue in our own lives. It's something that we need to develop and it's a lost reality that we need to steward well. If you have not received it yet, we are moving in that direction. Get ready! If you have received it, I invite you to rekindle the fire and draw from that glorious river within.

GLORIOUS REALITY

The apostle Paul gives us a preview of his devotional life: He prayed in tongues and highly valued the gift.

DISCUSSION QUESTIONS

What does Paul's example say to us—that he was a man who spoke in tongues frequently and was grateful for the gift?

_____

_____

_____

_____

_____

_____

Based on what you have discovered so far, how do you believe praying in tongues could impact your private devotional life?

_____

_____

_____

_____

_____

_____

_____

PRAYER

Holy Spirit, I am grateful for all the gifts You have made available. Thank You for the example of Paul and for showing me how his walk with God was so powerfully enriched by praying in tongues. I desire the same thing, Holy Spirit. I long for more and know You satisfy!

Tongues—Reveal the Humility and Wisdom of God

"Assuredly, I say to you, unless you are converted and become as little children, you will by no means enter the kingdom of heaven." —Matthew 18:3

God's Kingdom is based on humility. The only way we enter His Kingdom and, in turn, abide in His Kingdom is through humility. And so it is with the glorious reality of speaking in tongues. Scripture tells us that God purposefully chooses weak, insignificant things to manifest His power through. So it is with speaking in tongues. It blows me away that God chooses to hide His most glorious realities in common, mundane, ugly, even offensive ways. Let's consider a few. To start, the coming of Jesus the Messiah—in a dirty, smelly stable in Bethlehem. The King of kings born like a pauper. Likewise, consider His death. He actually establishes His Kingdom by laying down His life. To the natural mind and human wisdom, it makes little sense. But then again, it's truly the glory of God to hide a matter and our glory to seek it out. Truly wise men sought His glory, journeying from a long distance to embrace the wisdom of God manifested in a manger. Just as the Messiah was birthed in humble conditions, God births His church through a bunch of untrained fishermen, acting drunk, speaking in other tongues.

I propose to you that before we specifically wrestle with speaking in tongues, we need to discover what we really believe about God, His wisdom, and His ways, as tongues is just one expression of how His Kingdom is released. It's amazing how God's mysteries are revealed through babblings. This is why tongues are so offensive to many people. It is a direct affront to our minds and to our natural reasoning. We will continue to stumble over Kingdom realities until we humble ourselves and embrace God's wisdom. This makes me think of the game of limbo—how low can *you* go?

In Matthew 18, Jesus wasn't just speaking of a spiritual conversion where we get saved. Our minds need to become converted as well. We need to embrace Kingdom paradigms. Yes, the Kingdom is one of success, victory, and power, but how we access these realities is through getting low. Our level of humility gauges what we experience and release of God's supernatural power. One of our IHOP worship leaders, Laura Hackett, wrote a song about how God's river rushes to low places. This is absolutely true. We must humble ourselves to God's wisdom and methods, completely surrendering to His way of doing things.

GLORIOUS REALITY

We set ourselves up to experience the supernatural power of Holy Spirit when we assume a position of humility, surrendering ourselves to the wisdom and ways of God.

DISCUSSION QUESTIONS

Are there certain things about God's wisdom that offend or confuse you? List them below.

_____

_____

_____

_____

·

_____

_____

Are you using the gift of tongues in a regular way to access the life and wisdom of God? If not, why?

_____

_____

_____

_____

_____

_____

PRAYER

Holy Spirit, I humble myself before Your ways and Your wisdom. It may not make sense or compute with my natural way of thinking, but I want to receive everything You have. I desire to be a low place that receives the fullness of Your rushing river.

UNDERSTANDING THE DIFFERENT EXPRESSIONS OF TONGUES

*"Then there appeared to them divided tongues, as of fire,
and one sat upon each of them. And they were all filled
with the Holy Spirit and began to speak with other tongues,
as the Spirit gave them utterance."* —Acts 2:3-4

CAN YOU IMAGINE WHAT THAT SOUND OF MIGHTY RUSHING WIND sounded like? How about seeing divided tongues of fire resting over each one's head? After ten days in an upper room obeying Jesus' command to tarry in the city, the Promise of the Father was released on the day of Pentecost and all of history has been changed from that day forward. The thing that so shocks me is that, at the center of this historic moment, God places the tongues of all the nations on these disciples and they began to speak in these languages supernaturally, while everyone who was there heard these fishermen speaking their language. Jesus told us this would happen in Mark 16:17: *"And these signs will follow those who believe: In My name they will cast out demons; they will speak with new tongues."* Tongues are a sign that follows believers. Special believers? Apostles? Super spiritual people? No. It is a sign that follows believers. Period. If you are a believer, you are a prime candidate to receive and, in turn, exercise the gift of tongues.

The New Testament describes three different expressions of speaking in tongues. 1) There is the spiritual gift of delivering a message in tongues, which is accompanied by an interpretation. This is the prophetic expression of tongues Paul is describing in 1 Corinthians 12. 2) There is an evangelistic expression of tongues, where someone shares a message in a known tongue, but it is unknown to and unlearned by the person speaking. We read about this in Acts 2:3-4 as this manifestation of tongues saw the disciples speaking in different *known* languages. 3) The focus of this video series is the personal, devotional act of praying in tongues.

I want you to know right now that through the glorious gift of speaking in tongues, you can talk straight to your Father in heaven.

GLORIOUS REALITY

The gift of tongues was the single sign of the day of Pentecost and the outpouring of Holy Spirit.

DISCUSSION QUESTIONS

Have you received your prayer language before? Discuss.

_____

_____

_____

_____

_____

_____

How does the explanation of three different "kinds of tongues" help you?

_____

_____

_____

PRAYER

Holy Spirit, I ask for increased wisdom and understanding about how the gift of tongues is released. Show me the value of this glorious language and stir my heart to pursue it in a greater measure than ever before. If this is going to improve my relationship with You, then I want it all!

PREPARE FOR A
FRESH FILLING

"And do not get drunk with wine, for that is debauchery; but ever be filled and stimulated with the [Holy] Spirit. Speak out to one another in psalms and hymns and spiritual songs, offering praise with voices [and instruments] and making melody with all your heart to the Lord." —Ephesians 5:18-19 AMP

EVERYBODY GETS DRUNK ON SOMETHING. THIS IS EXACTLY WHAT PAUL IS talking about in Ephesians 5:18. *Drunk* is being underneath the control of something. Paul is making the point: Whose control will you be underneath? God's or the world's? How we satisfy this craving to be *filled* or *under the influence* can often be wrong, but the desire in and of itself was wired into us by God Himself. We were made to be filled with something—continually. God desired and created us to thirst. He made us a thirsty people, and that thirst will be quenched by *something*. The ultimate fulfillment of that thirst is satisfied in the Person of Holy Spirit. It is an ongoing, ever-increasing reality that we must pursue throughout our lives.

Holy Spirit is not some badge of honor we wear to broadcast our level of spirituality. It does not matter what you encountered 5, 10, 20 years ago at youth camp or during a revival service. Is the river of God flowing fresh in your life today? If not, I want to invite you to come and drink deep. In Ephesians 5, Paul is literally talking about a continuous life-style of being *filled* with the Holy Spirit. The Amplified version is most accurate when capturing the original Greek. It would be like saying, "Be *being* filled with the Spirit." It is not a one-time, fall on the floor, speak in tongues for a season and then on to the next thing type of experience. As we begin to make room for Holy Spirit to fill us, we can take some practical steps. Paul gives us one of these as he refers to *speaking out to one another* through spiritual songs. When we sing the Word of God and sing in tongues, we are taking some practical steps toward living a life continually filled with Holy Spirit. As we are filled, we will then begin to see breakthroughs in our lives; the Word of God will come alive like never before; and we will enjoy greater demonstrations of God's presence, power, and character made manifest through our lives.

GLORIOUS REALITY

We don't receive Holy Spirit one time and then move on to the next thing in our Christian walk. Holy Spirit is our Christian walk, and we must pursue continuous fresh fillings by His Presence and power.

DISCUSSION QUESTIONS

Are you currently living a *filled* life with Holy Spirit? If not, what are some ways you could reposition yourself to enjoy a fresh filling of His Presence and power in your life?

_____

_____

_____

_____

_____

_____

PRAYER

Fill me up, Holy Spirit. I celebrate what's happened in my past, but I want to experience You now. I am hungry for more. I have received Your fullness—because You live inside of me—but I want to experience it in my life. I'm not content just knowing I am filled—I desire to experience Your continuous filling!

Week Five

Benefits of Praying in the Spirit: How to Unlock the Revelatory Realm of Heaven over Your Life

VIDEO STUDY

Benefits of Praying in the Holy Spirit:

Benefit #1:   You are talking directly to _____. You have a
                _____ point in prayer. Two points of focus:

1.   God on the _____.

2.   God in my _____.

Benefit #2: You become open to the spirit
            of _____over your life.

You Are Speaking Four Main Realities:

1.   _____ about God.

2.   Truths about _____.

3.   The _____ of God's heart.

4.   People and situations that
     need _____.

Benefit #3: You embrace the _____ of Christ.

Benefit #4: Tongues is a _____ gift.

Benefit #5: You experience _____ kinds of prayer.

Benefit #6: You receive new confidence and _____ in prayer.

WHO ARE YOU REALLY TALKING TO?

"For he who speaks in a tongue does not speak to men but to God...." —1 Corinthians 14:2

THIS WEEK, I WANT US TO LOOK AT SEVERAL BENEFITS THAT COME FROM praying in Holy Spirit. Perhaps the most powerful, if not the most instrumental, is the fact that by praying in the Spirit, we are *talking directly to God*. This takes our understanding of intimacy with Him to a whole other dimension. Keep in mind, while praying in tongues you are not communicating with people, nor are you talking with demons. You are speaking *directly* to the Father. This is very important to keep in mind, as some mistakenly believe that by opening themselves up to praying in the Spirit, they are thereby opening a gateway to the demonic realm in their life. This is a great lie of the deceiver, for the last thing the enemy wants you doing is enjoying spirit-to-Spirit fellowship with God. He is well aware of the benefits that come from it. In fact, later on, we will discover how praying in the Spirit is actually an offensive weapon when it comes to donning the armor of God and engaging *offensive* spiritual warfare.

Beloved, you can be confident that when you are praying in another tongue, your spirit is speaking directly to God. No hindrances. No obstructions. No barriers. You and God are in communication as you pray in Holy Spirit. What a blessing and incredible benefit. When we pray in tongues we are exchanging intimacies with the Creator of the Universe. *Absolutely incredible!* This truth has so stabilized my prayer life. Many times in prayer, my mind wanders every five seconds. Reminding myself that I'm talking to God has increased my times of connection with Him. One of the things that I love to do is to have focal points of God when I pray. I love to picture God on the throne as described in Revelation 4 and God in my spirit as described in Colossians 1:27. Whenever my mind wanders, instead of getting beat up, I just simply bring my mind back to the focal point and continue to fellowship with God. Hardly anyone has any access to any president, king, or leader, but through the blood of Jesus and Holy Spirit, you and I have direct access to the President of the Universe!

GLORIOUS REALITY

When you pray in tongues, you are speaking directly to God!

DISCUSSION QUESTIONS

What does it mean that speaking in tongues gives you a direct phone line to the Creator of the Universe?

_____

_____

_____

_____

_____

Why is it important to remember that you are praying *directly* to God when you pray in tongues? How do you think this keeps you focused and centered in prayer?

_____

_____

_____

_____

_____

_____

_____

Prayer

Holy Spirit, thank You for making a way for me to have a direct, intimate connection with the Father. I am not speaking to men. I am not opening myself up to ungodly experiences. I am talking, spirit to Spirit, with God.

DEALING WITH THE DISTRACTIONS

"For if I pray in a tongue, my spirit prays, but my understanding is unfruitful." —1 Corinthians 14:14

DISTRACTIONS BECOME A NORMAL PART OF LIFE WHEN WE GIVE OUR-selves to extended times of praying in tongues. I want to address this subject, openly and authentically, as I believe so many people have given up on this gift because of these hindrances and distractions. In the following days, I'll give you some practical tools to help you persevere and remain focused. The key to developing praying in tongues as a normal part of life is pressing through the distractions. We cannot give up. In fact, I recommend giving it six months to a year, long term. Remember, this is all about developing a lifestyle that makes room for extended times of praying in tongues. This is not religious obligation—this is a super-natural gift that produces so many benefits in our lives. I have found that after 25 minutes of praying in tongues, things start to shift. I've noticed over the past 15 years of doing this that my mind begins to clear, the Word of God begins to open, divine thoughts come, I begin to feel what Holy Spirit is feeling, I receive new prayers and experience a wonderful sense of connection and centering in on the life of God. This doesn't happen 100 percent of the time, but it happens many, many times, and I've come to expect it.

Tomorrow, I am going to share two focal points that have helped me rein in my mind while praying. In the meantime, I want you to understand that praying in the Spirit represents a shift in how we are accustomed to praying, and I believe one of the most important things that takes place is a major transition in maturity. We truly discover what it means to press in and press past. We press into God, pressing past the distractions that try to get us off course. I've learned through praying in tongues for these times to train my mind and emotions and bring them into divine alignment. I tell people all the time that if I prayed or specifically prayed in tongues when I felt like it, then I would pray once a month. It's an act of obedience that brings about change. We must move from "feeling like it." Many times our circumstances, emotions, thoughts, and body can keep us from praying, but we must settle it that it's going to be a pull but our spirits will arise and run the day.

GLORIOUS REALITY

When you pray in tongues, your spirit—under the direct influence of Holy Spirit—takes the lead in your prayer life.

DISCUSSION QUESTIONS

I encourage you to write down the thoughts that come into your mind while you are praying in tongues. (Don't get discouraged by any of them. Be honest, as praying in tongues is like clearing out the dust in your interior life. Some thoughts may come up because Holy Spirit is doing a work and taking you to new levels in your relationship with Him.)

_____

_____

_____

_____

_____

_____

_____

_____

_____

_____

_____

_____

_____

_____

PRAYER

Holy Spirit, I ask You to take the lead in my prayer life. Empower me not to lean on my own understanding, to persevere through distractions, and to press in for all that You have available.

FOCAL POINT #1: GOD ON THE THRONE

"Immediately I was in the Spirit; and behold, a throne set in heaven, and One sat on the throne." —Revelation 4:2

OVER THE NEXT TWO DAYS, I AM GOING TO DESCRIBE TWO FOCAL POINTS that serve as anchors as I am praying in tongues. These are images that I focus on to keep my mind grounded and free from distractions. As I pray in tongues, there are two places that I focus my attention—upward and inward. Today, I want to discuss the upward focus where I fix my gaze upon the scene described in Revelation 4—God on the throne. This is the first place that Jesus took His disciples when giving them a model prayer. He directed them toward their Father in heaven. We cannot make this some "out there" reality. What's currently happening in heaven is very real and very relevant. We must become connected with the culture and environment of heaven's throne room because even though we are here on earth, our spirit has a place of residence in heavenly places, as Paul describes in Ephesians (see Eph. 2:6). We are on earth, but are also privileged to gaze upon the glorious throne room realities of heaven.

While praying in tongues, I try to focus on what's taking place in heaven, right now, and actually enter this glorious sanctuary and join the symphony of worship. Close your eyes and begin praying in tongues. Remember, this throne room encounter was not just limited to John. It was not just his experience—it is your inheritance in Christ. There's an open door for you to enter and "come up" to participate in this majestic scene. Look upon the One on the throne. Visualize His beauty like jasper. Take your place as one standing upon the sea of glass. Hear the thunderings. See the lightning. I encourage you to read this chapter in your Bible over and over, as it becomes a clearer picture for your mind to gaze upon while praying in tongues.

GLORIOUS REALITY

By fixing our gaze upon the glorious throne room of heaven, we give our minds a clear point of focus while praying in tongues.

DISCUSSION QUESTION

Why do you think it is so important to have clear "focal points" while you are praying in tongues?

_____

_____

_____

_____

_____

PRAYER EXERCISE

Read Revelation 4 out loud before praying in tongues. Capture the imagery of what is happening in heaven before you begin praying.

FOCAL POINT #2: GOD IN YOUR SPIRIT

"...Christ in you, the hope of glory." —Colossians 1:27

THE CREATOR OF HEAVEN AND EARTH LIVES INSIDE OF YOU! THE GOD OF all glory lives within your spirit. His power, His Presence, His resources, His life—His glory lives inside of us. As we move to our second focal point, we are invited to turn within and start accessing this glory. In the same way that I like to focus on God on the throne, I also focus on God in my spirit. This is the second focal point that I encourage you to have while praying in tongues. Here, you are setting your eyes on the burning fire of God living on the inside of you. One of the best things you can do with this focal point is awe and provoke yourself with questions. Did you know that the Shekinah glory of God lives inside of you? How is it possible that the God of Genesis 1:1—who could not be contained by any earthly structure—made a decision to dwell inside of you, and your physical frame remains *intact*? Questions like these are a doorway into revelation, as Holy Spirit is the One who will come and start releasing supernatural answers and insight.

One of the clearest pictures of this focal point in action is found in 2 Corinthians 3. Starting in verse 7, Paul starts blowing our minds as he compares the glory of the Old Covenant to what we have received through the Spirit. I feel like Paul is calling us to start tapping in to the glorious inheritance that lives on the inside, and the way he does this is by giving us a focal point to "behold." Verse 18 is key, as Paul notes that *"we all, with unveiled face, beholding as in a mirror the glory of the Lord, are being transformed into the same image from glory to glory, just as by the Spirit of the Lord"* (2 Cor. 3:18).

I encourage you to take time and slow down today. Focus on Holy Spirit living inside of you. Set your mind on Him. When you wander, come back to Him. The Man Christ Jesus lives in you by Holy Spirit, and by *beholding* Him you are being transformed *into His image.*

Glorious Reality

While praying in tongues, focus on the reality of God living inside of your spirit. The Genesis 1 Creator God resides in your mortal body, and by focusing on this reality, you are transformed by His glory into His image.

Discussion Activity/Prayer Directives

Take this opportunity to read 2 Corinthians 3:7-18. Go through it slowly, allowing yourself to be challenged by some of the concepts Paul is talking about.

Pray through these topics and discuss them with Holy Spirit. Write down what He shares with you about the Scriptures that stand out to you:

_____

_____

_____

_____

_____

_____

_____

UNLOCK THE SPIRIT OF REVELATION

"For one who speaks in an [unknown] tongue speaks not to men but to God, for no one understands or catches his meaning, because in the [Holy] Spirit he utters secret truths and hidden things [not obvious to the understanding]." —1 Corinthians 14:2 AMP

PAUL MAKES AN AMAZING STATEMENT HERE—WHEN WE SPEAK IN tongues, we are speaking *secret truths* and *hidden things*. Other translations call them *mysteries* (NKJV). These mysteries are not hidden from us, but hidden for us. Tongues are a supernatural way for us to access these mysteries, discover what God is saying, and experience the spirit of revelation in our lives. Remember—in God's Kingdom, hunger is a key currency. The mysteries, secrets, and hidden truths of heaven are hidden *for* the hungry. They are reserved for those who desire for and thirst after God. These are truths about God, us, our destinies, and about the plans and purposes of His heart. Think about with whom you share secrets and hidden truth. The deep plans and purposes of your heart are not public display—they are reserved for those you are most intimate with, right? God is the same way. The great invitation is that all of us have the ability to be intimate with Him and discover His mysteries. Mathew 13:11 makes it clear, as Jesus says, *"It has been given to you to know the mysteries of the kingdom of heaven."* There's but one question: *Who will humble him or herself to embrace the wisdom and ways of God when it comes to unlocking His mysteries?*

When we pray in tongues, divine revelation starts flowing out of God's realm and into me. In essence, I am building a "landing strip" for the spirit of revelation. I'm praying, "Holy Spirit, come land here—in my spirit—with the Word of God." This can happen in many ways. When we give ourselves to praying in the Spirit for extended periods of time, we begin to access the spirit of revelation in different ways. The still small voice of Holy Spirit gets clearer and clearer; our confidence in hearing God's voice increases; our dream life increases; visions become more prevalent; we become open to receiving words of knowledge, wisdom, and prophecy; and finally, God begins to speak to us about people in need. In fact, I believe Holy Spirit will begin to show you strategic people to pray for, give you names and specific instructions on how to pray for them, and even set up situations to where you will bump into those people who need ministry and you will have a *due season* word for them.

Glorious Reality

By praying in the Spirit, you open yourself up to the revelatory realm in greater ways that before.

Discussion Questions

Have you ever experienced hidden truths being revealed to you by Holy Spirit? If so, how?

_____

_____

_____

_____

Ask Holy Spirit to speak to you about how He can use you to bless others. Write down what He begins to share. (He might give you specific names, situations, information, etc.) Write these things down and begin to pray through them, asking for clarity.

_____

_____

_____

_____

_____

PRAYER

Holy Spirit, thank You for giving me access into the revelatory realm through praying in tongues. Thank You for an increase of words of knowledge, words of wisdom, and the gift of prophecy flowing out of my life to minister to others.

Week Six

Benefits of Praying in the Spirit: Keys to Building Up Your Inner Man

Week Six

VIDEO STUDY

Keys to Building Yourself Up in the Spirit:

Key #1: Understand that speaking in tongues is not a _____ type.

Key #2: When you pray in tongues, you _____ yourself.

Key #3: Praying in tongues builds up your _____ man.

    1.   Being strong in Spirit is becoming conformed into the likeness of _____.

    2.   Where your _____ goes, your soul and body will follow.

Key #4: Praying in tongues delivers you from the god of _____.

Key #5: Praying in tongues builds a highway for God's _____ on the inside of you.

    1.   We will go only as far as we are willing to go _____.

Key #6: Praying in tongues fosters divine _____ in the Spirit.

Key #7: Praying in tongues directs our focus to the _____ life.

THE IMPORTANCE OF YOUR INTERIOR LIFE

*"God judges persons differently than humans
do. Men and women look at the face; God looks
into the heart."* —1 Samuel 16:7 MSG

ONE OF OUR WORSHIP LEADERS, MISTY EDWARDS, WROTE A SONG describing where our real lives actually unfold—behind the face. This is the interior life. In this day and age, we have become absolutely consumed with externals. We are a generation that defines success by "how big" and "how much" and "how many," and God defines success in a completely different way. The Body of Christ is no exception. We can become guilty of focusing so much on the size of our influence over the size of our hearts that we end up losing both. When God made this statement to Samuel, He was making it clear that heaven is looking at our hearts, and that is what we are defined by. What did God see in this young shepherd boy? He saw a future king who was just as content before God and some sheep as he was leading the whole nation of Israel as king. His reward was *God*.

In the same way that God trained David on the back sides of the hills of Bethlehem, so I believe God is training a generation in this hour that will get lost before the "audience of One." And in the same way that this young man came to the forefront to take on and kill Goliath, so

God is going to bring forth a generation that has built up their interior lives, experienced breakthroughs in their soul, and has become positioned to step into places of leadership in the coming days to take on the end-time Goliaths.

How does all of this connect to praying in tongues? I'm glad you asked! Praying in tongues is one of the most powerful and practical ways we can build our interior lives. When praying in tongues, we are connecting with the only "eyes" in the world that matter—God's. Also, we are removing all the debris in our souls that hinder the life of God from flowing in and through us. As the coming rains of glory and crisis come, we will be able to stand and navigate through them instead of being destroyed because we have invested in building what is more important.

GLORIOUS REALITY

God does not see like man sees, for rather than evaluating based on the outside, He evaluates based on the condition of our interior lives.

DISCUSSION QUESTIONS

Why do you think the interior life of a person is so important to God? How was this the case with David (contrasted with King Saul)?

_____

_____

_____

_____

List some ways that praying in tongues builds up your interior life.

_____

_____

_____

PRAYER

Holy Spirit, help me to live from the inside out. May I be one like David, investing first and foremost in my devotional life with You, for everything else springs from that place.

You Are God's Building Project

"You are God's building." —1 Corinthians 3:9 NLT

JUST IMAGINE THE HIGH PRICE THAT IS PAID BY THOSE WHO DO NOT GIVE a natural building a solid foundation. Be it a house or skyscraper—it could be the most beautiful, eye-pleasing structure on the planet. However, appearance won't make any difference when the elements come and threaten the actual stability of the building. Let me put it this way. A building can be thousands of feet wide, but only inches deep. Depth is everything when it comes to developing sturdy foundations, and ultimately, establishing a structure that will be unshakeable when the elements come. I believe the Lord is delivering many of us from focusing primarily on the width or the "reach" of our lives and is focusing us in on the depth of our lives to be able to weather the coming days.

Paul says in 1 Corinthians 14:4 that when we pray in tongues, we "edify" ourselves. That word *edify* comes from the same Latin root as *edifice,* which means a "massive, magnificent building." As we pray for extended times in tongues, we are erecting, strengthening, and solidifying the building called our interior life to house and steward the life of God within us. In the same way you need to insert your computer charger into a source of electricity to receive power for your computer, so it is with praying in tongues. When we pray in tongues, we are plugging our interior life into the power of the indwelling Holy Spirit. I love all of the different things that I receive from other people, but I can edify myself. I can strengthen myself in God. Jude calls it "building ourselves up on our most holy faith" (see Jude 1:20). I'm convinced that if you will begin to set apart 25 minutes every day to focus on God and pray in the Holy Spirit, you will see the Master Builder go to work—even at an accelerated pace—in your life. Try it. *I dare you!*

GLORIOUS REALITY

As you pray in tongues, you are being built up into a supernatural structure with strong foundations and steadfastness through the trials and storms of life.

DISCUSSION QUESTIONS

What is your understanding of being (and becoming) *God's building*?

_____

_____

_____

_____

_____

How do you think praying in tongues helps build your faith?

_____

_____

_____

_____

_____

PRAYER

Holy Spirit, thank You for building the very life of God inside of me. You are the same Spirit who was inside of Jesus, helping Him to build a powerful and intimate devotional life with the Father. I believe You are doing the same thing with me, right now.

Edifying Yourself

"He who speaks in a tongue edifies him-self...."—1 Corinthians 14:4

We are living in a day where personal fitness and health is becoming a more and more common thing. I love it and am seeking to embrace it in my life as well as in my family. But at the same time, I'm convinced that if we were as focused on the current state of our interior life as we were our exterior life, we would see an explosion of revival break out all over the church. There are many believers who look like Arnold Schwarzenegger on the outside and yet look like Minnie Mouse on the *inside*. The number one thing that produces strength when working out is resistance. It's the resistance of the weight that produces strength and tone. It's the same way with praying in tongues. One of the things that you will find out quickly as you launch into a journey of extended times of praying in tongues is the resistance that you will face within your own soul. The pull of our nature is toward complacency, apathy, and laziness, and it's through praying in tongues that we "swim against the current" of our emotions and feelings. It's in this place that we become mighty in spirit!

John the Baptist was in the wilderness and "he became strong in spirit." He didn't become strong in personality, charisma, or even gifting, but he became strong in spirit. Becoming mighty in spirit is, in my opinion, the greatest need of the hour. In Ephesians 3, Paul prayed that we "would be strengthened with might in your inner man," and in Colossians 1 he prayed that we "would be strengthened with all might according to His glorious power." Paul understood that interior might is the great need to walk out a Christian life filled with joy and peace through every season of life. I'm convinced that the power of praying in tongues for extended periods of time has connected my inner man to the riches of *His* power and glory that resides within me. As I break through all of my changing emotions and wandering thoughts, accessing the light and power of God within me, I'm strengthened from the inside out and it radically changes my thought life, emotional chemistry, and desires.

GLORIOUS REALITY

As we pray in tongues, we strengthen our inner man and receive the glorious power and light of God.

DISCUSSION QUESTIONS

Have you discovered the resistance within your own soul as you have sought to pray in tongues for extended periods of time? Describe.

_____

_____

_____

_____

_____

PRAYER

Thank You, Holy Spirit, that You are strengthening and building up my inner man as I pray in tongues.

Day Four

YOU ARE LED BY THE SPIRIT

*"For as many as are led by the Spirit of God,
these are sons of God." —*Romans 8:14

GOD HAS DESIGNED US INTENTIONALLY—BODY, SOUL, AND SPIRIT. JUST as the tabernacle contained the outer court, the inner court, and the Holy of Holies, so God has built us in the same way. The outer court is our body, the inner court is our soul (mind, will, and emotions), and the Holy of Holies is our spirits. The day you are born again, the very glory of God takes up residence within your spirit. That which was once dead is now alive by the Spirit of God. God has designed you in such a way that the reality within your spirit would transform the reality in your soul and body. As we spend extended times praying in tongues, the life of God in our spirits coupled with the Word of God begins to spring up, changing over time our thought lives, emotional chemistry, desires, and even our physical bodies. Paul stated in Romans 8:11 that *"the Spirit of Him who raised Jesus from the dead dwells in you, He who raised Christ from the dead will also give life to your mortal bodies through His Spirit who dwells in you."* That's amazing that the resurrection power of God resides in me and has the potential to give life and power to my physical body.

Paul stated a few verses later that *"as many as are led by the Spirit of God, these are sons of God"* (Rom. 8:14). Think about it what it means to be "led by the Spirit." You can also put in the word *governed* or *under the leadership*. Many times, I'm more led by my soul than I am by my spirit. The circumstances that come my way throw my thought life and emotions into a swirl and I lose my way. When we pray in tongues, we are in essence telling our soul to get into the backseat and our spirit to get into the driver's seat. My desire is that my spirit man would lead the way. This doesn't mean that bad circumstances and situations won't come my way. What it does mean is that I can have divine perspective in the middle of the storms of life. *Perspective is everything.*

GLORIOUS REALITY

We were designed by God to be led by our spirits and that this would impact every other area of our lives.

DISCUSSION QUESTIONS

How does praying in tongues relate to being "led by the Spirit"? How have you experienced this in your life?

_____

_____

_____

_____

_____

Have you experienced the fruit of being led by the Spirit in difficult circumstances? What was the fruit you experienced?

_____

_____

_____

_____

_____

PRAYER

Holy Spirit, because I am a son/daughter of God, it is my inheritance to be Spirit-led and directed by You. You go before me; You are behind me. You are with me. Thank You for always speaking, and for increasing my sensitivity to Your voice as I pray in the Spirit.

Day Five

PREPARING A HIGHWAY
FOR HIS GLORY

"Prepare the way of the Lord; make straight in the desert a highway for our God. Every valley shall be exalted and every mountain and hill brought low; the crooked places shall be made straight and the rough places smooth; the glory of the Lord shall be revealed, and all flesh shall see it together...." —Isaiah 40:3-5

IN THE SAME WAY THAT GOD RAISED UP JOHN THE BAPTIST TO "GO before" the first coming of Jesus, God is raising up forerunners all over the earth who are being called forth to prepare the earth for the second coming of Jesus. Before they come forth to prepare this highway in the earth, they must first learn how to cooperate with Holy Spirit in the preparation of the highway within their own hearts. Can you imagine all of the demolition and clearing that is involved in building a highway? I remember a highway being built near my hometown when I was growing up, and when the highway came to a huge mountain, the only thing they could do to make a way through the mountain was to use dynamite to clear it out. This is literally the picture that I get when giving myself to extended times of praying in tongues. I'm seeking to see the glory within released into my thought life, emotional chemistry, and body, but it must demolish, destroy, and remove existing strongholds, arguments, and emotions that exalt themselves against the knowledge of God.

139

One of the greatest realities that I believe praying in tongues has taught me is cultivating the "breaker anointing" in my life. When those times of resistance rise up within me, I lean in knowing that God is the God of the breakthrough, and that small breakthroughs today are training me for big breakthroughs tomorrow. Through praying in tongues and the word of God, you will begin to see the valleys of shame and guilt raised up. You will begin to see the mountains of pride and independence brought low. You will begin to see the crooked places of distortion straightened, and all the rough places of religion and harshness made smooth. Why is all this happening? So that the glory of the Lord would be revealed in us and through us. This is our inheritance

GLORIOUS REALITY

Praying in tongues prepares a highway within our souls for the glory of God.

DISCUSSION QUESTIONS

How is John the Baptist an example to us today when it comes to building up our interior lives by praying in Holy Spirit?

_____

_____

_____

_____

In what ways can you become stronger and more well-built in your spirit?

_____

_____

_____

PRAYER

Holy Spirit, continue to enlarge my capacity to carry and release Your Presence. Increase the strength of my spirit, that You would reign in every area of my life and that my spirit would be under Your direct influence and government. Holy Spirit, You are Lord of my spirit and I pray that every other area of my life would fall under that reign.

Week Seven

Waging Victorious Spiritual Warfare

VIDEO STUDY

Level One Warfare: Supernatural Strategies for Winning the Interior Battle

1. _____: The essential part you play in releasing victory over your life.

2. You will walk in the Spirit to the degree that you _____ in the Spirit.

3. Be mindful that the flesh is always _____; you don't graduate from the battle.

4. You don't have to give in to the _____ of your flesh.

5. Holy Spirit came to _____ you into the image of Jesus Christ.

Level Two Warfare: Supernatural Strategies for Engaging Offensive Warfare

Praying in tongues is a practical way to put on your spiritual _____.

1. Your two offensive weapons:

   a. The Sword of the Spirit: The _____ of God.

b. _____ in the Spirit.

2. When you pray in the Spirit, you are strengthened to
_____ the sword of the Spirit.

3. Building a defense system around your life can _____
assignments from the enemy.

4. We must have a bridal identity and a
warfare _____.

Day One

ENLISTED FOR WARFARE

"Fight the good fight of faith...."—1 Timothy 6:12

THIS WEEK, WE ARE GOING TO LOOK AT THE POWER OF TONGUES AS IT pertains to the call to daily warfare against the schemes of the devil from within and without. We are called to war, not from a place of trying to accomplish victory, but from a place of standing on the victory of the finished work of the cross. Through Jesus' death and resurrection, the powers of hell were disarmed, and the keys of hell were taken. We who were once dead were set free from sin and death and raised up with Him and seated together with Him in the heavenly places to join Him and execute the finished work. Many believers will just conclude that Jesus did everything for me, so I don't have to do anything, yet Paul repeated many times in the Epistles to believers that they must "fight" and "wage the good warfare." First Peter 5:8 states that the devil walks about like a roaring lion, seeking whom he may devour. Our response to this is not to become fearful, but to be sober, aware, and not ignorant of the enemy's schemes.

God has given us two massive weapons in this war, and they are the Word of God coupled with praying in Holy Spirit. These two weapons, when used, bring change to the greatest place of warfare—our minds. As we pray in tongues and declare the Word of God, strongholds and arguments are dethroned in our hearts and minds, and we become renewed in truth. Many times these strongholds are the result of misunderstanding the finished work of the cross and the righteousness we now possess before the throne of God. Again, when we pray in tongues, the spirit of revelation is touching our hearts and minds and we are coming into truth. Stand strong today in what He's done and go to war!

GLORIOUS REALITY

We are called to war not from a place of defeat but from a place of victory.

DISCUSSION QUESTIONS

How have you seen or understood spiritual warfare in the life of believer? How do you engage in this war?

_____

_____

_____

_____

_____

Are you currently experiencing any measure of warfare in your life? What kind is it—*internal* (going on in the inside of you) or *external* (dealing with the enemy)?

_____

_____

_____

_____

_____

In the days ahead, we are going to discover how to use praying in tongues as an offensive weapon against both internal and external forces that are coming against you.

PRAYER

Holy Spirit, You equip me to live in sustained, consistent victory. Thank You for tools and strategies to exercise authority over my flesh and the devil. In the days to come, show me how I can use this wonderful gift of praying in tongues to build my spirit and wage warfare from the position of victory that Jesus paid for me to stand in.

PRAY IN THE SPIRIT AND PUT ON CHRIST

"But put on the Lord Jesus Christ, and make no provision for the flesh, to fulfill its lusts." —Romans 13:14

THERE IS ONE RAGING AROUND THIS PLANET LIKE A ROARING LION, looking for those he can devour (see 1 Pet. 5:8). In Romans 13, like many places in the New Testament, Paul calls us to "put on the Lord Jesus Christ." What exactly does that mean? I thought He was already on me. One of the most practical ways that I've found to obey this verse is through extended times of praying in tongues. Over the last 15 years of regularly praying in tongues, I've found that around the 20 minute mark, my thoughts begin to change, my emotions begin to change, prayers start coming out of me, and I'm able to connect with God in an easier and more sustainable way. This is what I've come to understand "putting on the Lord Jesus Christ" to look like. It's stepping into the spirit, out of the soul. It's putting your spirit on the front seat of your bike and putting your soul on the back seat.

It's when we "put Him on" that we are empowered and equipped to live, walk, talk, and fellowship in the Spirit. When "He comes on me," I feel His thoughts, His emotions, His prayers, His faith move through me. Beloved, this is your inheritance—to be a conduit of the very life of Jesus Christ. So many believers live so below the poverty line of the Kingdom, and it's time for a generation to lay hold of the life of God residing within them. "Christ in you" is the answer to a thousand questions, circumstances, and difficulties. I dare you to set your heart, lift your eyes, and engage God by praying in tongues. Watch what happens!

GLORIOUS REALITY

We put on Christ and build up our spirits by praying in tongues. This empowers us to manifest Christ in the earth, rather than consistently falling prey to the desires and appetites of the flesh.

DISCUSSION QUESTIONS

What does it mean to you to "put on the Lord Jesus Christ"?

_____

_____

_____

_____

_____

What are some situations where you have seen His life manifested through you?

_____

_____

_____

_____

_____

PRAYER

Holy Spirit, continue to build my inner man. Empower me to put on Christ and make no provision for my flesh. As I pray in tongues, I believe that my spirit becomes stronger. As my spirit strengthens, I pray that ungodly desires and fleshly appetites completely lose their appeal to me.

THE WARFARE OF INTIMACY

"But I say, walk and live [habitually] in the [Holy] Spirit [responsive to and controlled and guided by the Spirit]; then you will certainly not gratify the cravings and desires of the flesh (of human nature without God)." —Galatians 5:16 AMP

I CANNOT THINK OF A CLEARER VERSE IN THE BIBLE THAT LAYS OUT THE secret to an effective, victorious, and happy Christian life. Paul gives us an amazing law in the Kingdom. He in essence tells us that if we walk in the Spirit, we will not fulfill the lusts of the flesh. This is absolutely astounding. If we walk in the Spirit, then we will not look at pornography or be gripped with jealousy, anger, rage, fear, shame. The power of sin will be inoperative because we are living in a different realm called "the Spirit." Yesterday, we looked at "putting on the Lord Jesus." Today, we are going to look at "walking in the Spirit." These two commands are the same command. They are the call to breakthrough out of our soul life and into our spirit life. Many believers never experience the inexhaustible riches of God residing on the inside and instead live defeated, anemic Christian lives. This is not what Jesus died for. He died that we would receive revelation of what we possess and then live a life of accessing this glory within.

How do you "walk in the Spirit"? The only way we will walk in the Spirit is by talking *to* the Spirit and talking *in* the Spirit. When we set our minds and hearts on the glory within and begin to draw on that life,

His love, joy, peace, etc. will bubble up, changing the atmosphere in our minds, emotions, and bodies. Several verses later in Galatians 5, Paul tells us that the fruit of the Spirit, or the fruit of fellowshipping in the Spirit, is "love, joy, peace, patience, kindness, goodness, faithfulness, gentleness, self-control." When we pray in tongues for extended periods of time, the fruit will be the above. This is the desire of God for every believer to live this life of manifesting the fruits of God. Everybody agrees that this is what God wants, but few of us practically know how to see this come about. Thanks be to God for the glorious gift of praying in tongues.

GLORIOUS REALITY

When we talk to the Spirit and talk in the Spirit, we walk in the Spirit and are empowered to not fulfill the lusts of the flesh.

DISCUSSION QUESTIONS

What are ways that your flesh has won because you didn't walk in the Spirit?

_____

_____

_____

_____

_____

How will intimacy with God empower you to experience victory over fleshly desires and appetites? In what ways can you begin to cultivate this intimacy?

_____

_____

_____

_____

_____

_____

_____

PRAYER

Holy Spirit, You empower me to enjoy new dimensions of intimacy with God. I am going to stop striving and fighting in my own strength to become holy and walk in victory over the flesh. Show me how to wage warfare from a position of intimacy. I pray that as I continue to draw near to You, the things of this world would lose their appeal to me.

YOUR OFFENSIVE WEAPONS

"The sword of the Spirit, which is the word of God. Pray in the Spirit at all times and on every occasion." —Ephesians 6:17-18 NLT

AFTER PAUL LISTS THE DIFFERENT PARTS OF THE ARMOR OF GOD FOR spiritual warfare in Ephesians 6:14-17, he concludes by sharing two offensive weapons. These two offensive weapons are the greatest and many times are the most underused weapons in the Christian life. They are the Word of God and praying in tongues for extended periods of time. These two weapons when put together are the greatest threats to the kingdom of darkness. The Word of God is so powerful. The heavens were made through the Word of God. Nations have been built and destroyed by the Word. The sick have been healed, the demonized delivered, the dead raised by the Word of God, and this Word is living on the inside of us and is right in front of us. However, it's when the Word of God is released through a mighty spirit that the force of the Word is felt.

When Jesus was in the wilderness being tempted by the devil, He fought the devil using the Word of God. When we build ourselves up through praying in the Spirit, the Word of God comes out of our spirit like a mighty sword cutting off the schemes of the evil one. Many believers will live under oppression, sickness, fear, etc. and never open their mouths and declare the Word of God. We must do our part and release the Word of God through song and declaration. We must go from a defensive posture of just waiting for things to happen to an offensive posture that builds a wall of fire around our lives and loved ones. I encourage you to take 25 minutes today to pray in the Spirit and declare the Word of God over those situations in your life that need breakthrough.

GLORIOUS REALITY

Praying in tongues is your key to transitioning from a defensive Christian life to an offensive one.

DISCUSSION QUESTIONS

What are some ways you have seen the power of the Word of God and praying in the Spirit work in your life?

_____

_____

_____

_____

_____

Are there any areas in your life that you need breakthrough in?

_____

_____

_____

_____

_____

PRAYER

Holy Spirit, I want to move beyond defensive warfare and start offensively releasing the Kingdom. I want to gain new territory and ground. Even if the enemy has had me trapped in a cycle, I break that now, in Jesus' Name, and begin wielding my offensive weapon of praying in the Spirit.

WARFARE FROM VICTORY

"Let the saints be joyful in glory; let them sing aloud on their beds. Let the high praises of God be in their mouth and a two-edged sword in their hand." —Psalms 149:5-6

THIS IS ONE OF THOSE GLORIOUS PASSAGES THAT GIVES US A SNEAK PEAK of what the church will look like in the generation of the Lord's return. We get to see in these verses the bringing together of joyful glory, singing from a place of rest the high praises of God, and at the same time a double-edged sword, which is the Word of God. As we spoke about on the first day, we don't fight from a place of trying to achieve victory, but from a place of already-received victory. Jesus won the victory 2,000 years ago at the cross, but we get to partner with Him in the execution of the written sentence against the devil and his kingdom. We are seated with Christ in heavenly places, and as we sing in the Spirit and as we sing the Word of God, He binds, He destroys, He delivers us from our enemies. What the devil attempted to get when he tried to usurp God's throne, God has freely given us through the death and resurrection of Jesus.

On this last day of the week, I want you to take a deep breath, fill your mind with thoughts of where you are now in the heavenly places, and begin to sing in the Spirit straight to the throne. As you do this, know that the atmosphere around you is being changed and that your enemies are being destroyed. Just as Jehoshaphat put the singers ahead of the army and God routed out their enemies, so God is raising up a people who will sing from a place of rest and watch God fight our battles for us.

GLORIOUS REALITY

Jesus conquered the powers of darkness so that, through Holy Spirit, you could fight from a position of victory.

DISCUSSION QUESTIONS

What does it mean to fight *from* victory instead of fighting *for* victory?

_____

_____

_____

_____

How does this concept change the way you will engage spiritual warfare in the future?

_____

_____

_____

_____

PRAYER

Holy Spirit, You empower me to enforce Jesus' victory in every situation. I am not fighting, trying to win. I am already victorious because of what Jesus accomplished. Because of this, I work with You, Holy Spirit, to see Jesus' victory recognized and enforced in every situation that is in disagreement with His Word and will.

Week Eight

How to Activate the Power of the Holy Spirit in Your Life

Video Study

1. Defining a religious spirit: Settling down and thinking you've _____.

2. _____ is the currency to God's Kingdom.

3. You are to be _____ filled with the Holy Spirit.

Keys to Receiving and Administering the Baptism of the Holy Spirit:

1. Calm down and _____.

2. Correct _____ ideas.

3. Pray _____ prayers.

4. Start _____ whatever comes out of your spirit.

5. Stop speaking in your _____ language.

6. Speak out _____ for five to ten minutes, and don't stop.

Breaking Through Hindrances:

1. Determine if there were any _____ stands taken against Holy Spirit.

2. Create a _____ environment.

3. Encourage people to keep _____ for tongues—even if they don't receive it immediately after they are prayed for.

THERE IS MORE AVAILABLE FOR YOU

"And I will pray the Father, and He will give you another Helper, that He may abide with you forever." —John 14:16

"...But tarry in the city of Jerusalem until you are en- dued with power from on high." —Luke 24:49

THERE IS SO MUCH MORE! I'M SO GRATEFUL FOR THE GIFT OF SALVATION and all that it entails. I'm so grateful for the life of the Spirit within me. I'm so grateful for the gift of tongues and all of the glorious benefits that have come into my life because of giving myself to it for years. In light of all of this, I want you to know there is more. Whether the "more" is something that comes from above or breaks out from within, I don't really care. I just know there is more. Jesus in a resurrected body spent 40 days with 500 people teaching on the Kingdom of God, and still that wasn't enough for them to begin Christianity. Out of 500, 380 of them thought that it was enough because only 120 made it to the upper room obeying Jesus' command to "wait for the promise of the Spirit." Throughout the book of Acts and throughout history, we see that there are ongoing, fresh baptisms of the Holy Spirit for greater witness and power in the earth. This is what I'm desperate for, and my prayer is that you would become hungry for the same reality in your life.

I'm sad to say that so many "Spirit-filled" believers have turned their prayer language into a badge of having arrived into the fullness of God, and have stopped reaching in their spiritual life for the fullness of God. In Ephesians 5, Paul commands us to go on being filled with Holy Spirit. His understanding is that it's not a one-time experience but an ever-increasing encounter with a Person who is bringing you into greater realms of intimacy and power. I believe that if we steward the gift of tongues, then God will open us up to greater gifts as well as greater realms of intimacy and power with Himself. This last week is about giving you a vision for the rest of your days here on earth of full immersion into God Himself. Begin to ask God to make you hungry for more. He loves to answer!

GLORIOUS REALITY

There is more to the Christian life than our current experience. However, it does not involve seeking out new information or even new revelation; it is accessing and activating the Person of Holy Spirit within us.

ACTIVATION JOURNAL

*For this week, instead of having you go through discussion questions, I would like you to record your experiences with Holy Spirit in the *Activation Journal.*

Are you aching for *more* in your Christian life? How do you think you can experience this through a deeper relationship with Holy Spirit?

_____

_____

_____

_____

_____

_____

_____

_____

_____

_____

_____

_____

_____

_____

_____

_____

_____

_____

_____

_____

_____

_____

_____

_____

PRAYER

Holy Spirit, show me how to access and release the more that is already on the inside of me.

Day Two

HE'S A GOOD FATHER

"...How much more will your Heavenly Father give the
Holy Spirit to those who ask Him!" —Luke 11:13

WHEN IT COMES TO RECEIVING FRESH BAPTISMS AND IMMERSIONS IN the life and power of Holy Spirit, you must understand that the Person you are asking is the kindest, most generous, most powerful Person you will ever meet. In Luke 11, Jesus gives us great confidence when asking God to fill us with Holy Spirit by letting us know that if we ask Him for bread, He will not give us a stone, but will give us the very thing that we are asking for. The second thing Jesus lets us know is that compared to God, we are all evil. No matter how good you think you are, all of us are evil compared to Father. Jesus said that if we, being evil, have the capacity to give good gifts to our own children, how much more will our heavenly Father give good gifts to His children?

He's not the kind of father who makes you go outside and work for eight hours before you can open your Christmas gifts, nor is He the kind of father who keeps hiding from you so that you can never find him. He draws us out through promises to ask Him, and it's when we ask, seek, and knock that doors open up. He is a good Father who is brilliant in His leadership in bringing us the fullness of His plan. He is gracious, compassionate, merciful, all powerful, all wise, all knowing, and He loves to give good gifts.

GLORIOUS REALITY

Our Father is so good and He loves to give Holy Spirit to those who ask Him.

ACTIVATION JOURNAL

Are there wrong thoughts about your Father in heaven that have hindered you from receiving fresh releases of Holy Spirit in your life? Discuss.

_____

_____

_____

_____

_____

_____

_____

_____

_____

_____

_____

PRAYER

I want to know the Father Jesus knew. Holy Spirit, unveil the heart and the nature of my Father and awaken faith in me to ask Him for the fullness of Holy Spirit.

THE KEY OF HUNGER

*"Blessed are you who hunger now, for you
shall be filled."* —Luke 6:21

IN HIS *SERMON ON THE MOUNT*, JESUS GAVE US THE TRUE DEFINITION of success and happiness in God's eyes. He spoke specifically about cultivating eight realities in our lives that God deems as "blessed." Among these is the blessing of hungering for righteousness. Hunger is the currency to the Kingdom. The whole Kingdom is accessed through hunger. If there is one principle that the gospel makes clear, it is this: Jesus simply does things for hungry people that He doesn't do for everyone else. The woman with the issue of blood, the Canaanite woman, and Blind Bartimaeus are all stories of people who pressed past all opposition, all fear and laid hold of Jesus and received that which they sought. Paul himself declared in Philippians 3 that he wanted to lay hold of that for which Jesus laid hold of him. You need to ask yourself this question: Why did Jesus lay hold of your life and save you? Paul's whole life was a violent, hungry search to discover the answer to this question.

One of my heroes in the faith in modern times is John G. Lake. There are many aspects of his life that are admirable, but the greatest one to me was a high vision for the life of God in man, which thereby released such an amazing hunger in this man's life. To him, greater intimacy with Jesus and power were one and the same thing. His longing was for greater nearness to God, which released greater realms of power, but his desire was greater proximity to Jesus. I have a question for you: Are you hungry for God? Honestly, are you hungry? Hunger is when a desire becomes the ultimate obsession in your life and until it is answered you will not be satisfied. Let us pray to get hungry.

GLORIOUS REALITY

Hunger for God is the currency to the Kingdom. Those who hunger will be filled.

ACTIVATION JOURNAL

Spend today honestly assessing your hunger. Ask yourself what are some of the areas that are stealing hunger from your life. What are some disciplines that you can do to enhance hunger in your life? Also, try to find some books on John G. Lake to read about his journey in hunger.

_____

_____

_____

_____

_____

_____

_____

PRAYER

Holy Spirit, I ask You to increase my hunger for the things of God in my life. Enlarge my capacity to both receive from You and release Your power to the world around me.

Day Four

JESUS THE BAPTIST

"He will baptize you with the Holy Spir-
it and fire." —Matthew 3:11

DURING THE VIDEO SESSION THIS WEEK, I GAVE AN INVITATION FOR YOU to be filled with Holy Spirit and speak in tongues. There will be some of you who will receive this for the first time and you will see a great change in your life. Some of you have received your prayer language, but what used to be a river flowing out of your belly is now a dam and has become dry. Whether this is your first time or if you've already experienced it before, I believe God wants to fill you afresh today with His fire and glory and change your life. Today, we cast off all of our badges and former experiences and simply ask God to fill us with His Holy Spirit. He is a good Father and He loves to give good gifts to His children. If you ask Him, He will answer you with the very thing you are desiring. You can never be good enough to receive it or work hard enough to earn it because it's a free gift. All you need to do is simply ask, open your heart, and receive. When you feel Him rising up within you, open your mouth and pray in Holy Spirit.

John the Baptist's favorite title for Jesus was *Jesus the Baptist.* In each of the four Gospels, John points to One who would come and provide a baptism that was far beyond what people were experiencing in water. He continually declared that there was One coming who would baptize you with Holy Spirit and fire. One of the primary missions of Jesus was to come, die, be raised again, ascend, and baptize the church with Holy Spirit and fire. This mission will become very clear in the coming days as we move into the greatest hour ever.

Today, let's ask for a fresh baptism—immersion into Holy Spirit. Open your heart and ask God for it. He will meet you.

GLORIOUS REALITY

Jesus died on the cross so you could be cleansed of sin and become baptized with Holy Spirit on earth. His redemptive work was not just about getting you into heaven, but about getting heaven into you through Holy Spirit.

ACTIVATION JOURNAL/PRAYER

Have you personally received the baptism of Holy Spirit? If not, I encourage you to keep praying the words I shared in the video session. Write down what Holy Spirit is saying/doing in this time of pursuit. If you have, ask yourself whether the baptism of Holy Spirit has become a "badge" in your life.

_____

_____

_____

_____

_____

_____

_____

_____

_____

_____

I encourage you to pray simple prayers when it comes to pursuing the baptism of Holy Spirit. Here's an example:

Jesus, You are the One who baptizes me with Holy Spirit.

Thank You for paying for my sin on the cross so that I could go to heaven and also receive heaven in my spirit now—the glorious Holy Spirit.

Father, I ask You to baptize me in Holy Spirit's power and Presence. Fill me to overflowing. I want to speak in tongues.

I want to operate in all of Holy Spirit's supernatural gifts and grow in both character and power as He conforms me into the image of Jesus.

After you pray these words, I encourage you to stop praying in your native language and wait on that stirring or upwelling of Holy Spirit inside of you. Begin to speak out in faith the words or syllables He deposits into your spirit. Remember, you have a part to play in the process too. God will not sovereignly overwhelm your mouth and move your lips—you need to step out and speak the words Holy Spirit is depositing in your heart.

Even if you receive a single word or syllable, celebrate it and start speaking it *out loud!*

THE SPIRIT AND THE BRIDE SAY, "COME!"

"And the Spirit and the bride say, 'Come!' And let him who hears say, 'Come!' And let him who thirsts come. Whoever desires, let him take the water of life freely." —Revelation 22:17

IN REVELATION 22:17, WE SEE AN AMAZING PROPHECY OF WHAT THE church will look like before the coming of the Lord. This verse contains three specific realities that will be manifested in the earth. The first thing is that there is coming a day when Holy Spirit and the church will come into unity with each other. God will release great glory and crisis in the earth for the purpose of joining His church with the agenda of Holy Spirit. He will shake everything that can be shaken so that we will awaken to everything He died for. For the last 2,000 years, the church has been on AM and Holy Spirit has been on FM, but there is coming a day when the very desires of Holy Spirit will become the desires of the church.

As the church and Holy Spirit come into unity with one another, Holy Spirit will begin to shift the identity of the church into a new identity and give us a new name—the Bride. Holy Spirit is emphasizing Jesus as the Bridegroom God, which will thereby change the way we see ourselves. This Bride will love what He loves and hate what He hates. She will be in full agreement with His will and purpose and will partner with Him in bringing His Kingdom to the earth.

This Bride will partner with the Bridegroom in the primary anointing that He is releasing on the end-time church—prayer. It will be the prayer, "Come," that will call Jesus back to the planet, to rapture the saints, judge the wicked, and save the nation of Israel.

How does all of this relate to tongues? I'm glad you asked! As we give ourselves to years and even decades of praying in the Spirit, we are brought into unity with His mind, will, and purpose, our identities are changed into bridal identity, and the anointing of prayer comes on our life with an increasing understanding of the end-time drama. Holy Spirit is awakening the church all over the earth from her slumber, and it will be through praying in tongues that the church will come into her greatest hour.

GLORIOUS REALITY

Holy Spirit will bring us into unity with Himself, giving us a new identity and anointing us with the spirit of prayer.

ACTIVATION JOURNAL

Write down what you want to see happen in your life over the next year, 5 years, 10 years, etc.

_____

_____

_____

_____

_____

_____

Thank you for joining me on this journey.

I pray that because of our time together, you are hungrier than ever before to experience the Person of Holy Spirit and release the powerful gift of praying in tongues.

Answer Key

Week One

1. salvation
2. What takes place at your salvation?
   a. DNA
   b. re-creation
   c. substance
   d. unsuccessful
   e. overcomes
   f. you
3. within

Week Two

Who Is Holy Spirit?

1. Person
2. God
3. upgrades
4. helper
5. Truth

6. forever

7. teacher

What Will Holy Spirit Do?

1. guide

2. authority

3. come

4. Jesus

5. reveal

Who Is Holy Spirit?

1. deep

2. age to come

Week Three

God's Divine Design for Communion:

1. communion

2. protocol

3. man

4. tabernacle

Three Keys to Understanding God's Design for Communion. You Have:

1. outer court

2. soul

3. spirit

How You Can Experience Communion with Holy Spirit:

1. structure

2. sanctified

3. engage

4. below

Tools to Experience Holy Spirit in Your Life:

1. Meditate, Questions

2. Fellowshipping

TRUST

Thank

Reign

Use

Strengthen

Teach

Week Four

Truths About Speaking in Tongues:

1. hurt

2. gateway

3. prophetic

4. Scripture

5. devotional

6. wisdom

7. church

Three Expressions of Tongues in the New Testament:

1. languages

2. gift

3. devotional

WEEK FIVE

Benefits of Praying in the Holy Spirit:

Benefit #1: God, focal

1. throne

2. spirit

Benefit #2: revelation.

You Are Speaking Four Main Realities:

1. truths

2. you

3. plans

4. breakthrough

Benefit #3: mind

Benefit #4: gateway

Benefit #5: new

Benefit #6: boldness

WEEK SIX

Keys to Building Yourself Up in the Spirit:

Key #1: personality

Key #2: edify

Key #3: inner

1. Christ

2. spirit

Key #4: convenience

Key #5: glory

1. deep

Key #6: unity

Key #7: interior

Week Seven

Level One Warfare: Supernatural Strategies for Winning the Interior Battle

1. Faith

2. talk

3. raging

4. demands

5. conform

Level Two Warfare: Supernatural Strategies for Engaging Offensive Spiritual Warfare

armor

1. Your two offensive weapons:

    a. Word

    b. Praying

2. use

3. cancel

4. mentality

WEEK EIGHT

1. arrived

2. Hunger

3. continually

Keys to Receiving and Administering the Baptism of the Holy Spirit:

1. relax

2. false

3. simple

4. speaking

5. natural

6. loud

Breaking Through Hindrances:

1. generational

2. light

3. asking

Website:
www.coreyrussell.org
Facebook:
Official-CoreyRussell
YouTube:
officialcoreyrussell
Twitter:
@brotherrussell
Contact:
info@coreyrussell.org

Other Products *from* Corey Russell

The External Glory of
an Intercessor DVD

Ancient Paths CD

Days of Noah CD

Eyes Opened CD

Pursuit of the Holy

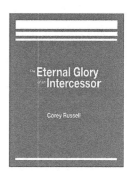

The External Glory of
an Intercessor
Study Guide

Made in the USA
Coppell, TX
12 February 2024

28902574R00108